The Power of Community:
Give, Get and Grow

The Power of Community: Give, Get, and Grow

Vaishali Mane

BEP

BUSINESS EXPERT PRESS

Leader in applied, concise business books

The Power of Community: Give, Get, and Grow

First published in 2025 by
Business Expert Press, LLC
222 East 46th Street, New York, NY 10017
www.businessexpertpress.com

ISBN-13: 978-1-63742-838-2 (paperback)
ISBN-13: 978-1-63742-839-9 (e-book)

Business Expert Press Collaborative Intelligence Collection

First edition: 2025

10 9 8 7 6 5 4 3 2 1

EU SAFETY REPRESENTATIVE
Mare Nostrum Group B.V.
Mauritskade 21D
1091 GC Amsterdam
The Netherlands
gpsr@mare-nostrum.co.uk

Description

The Power of Community: Give, Get, and Grow is a heartfelt reflection of the values of generosity and selflessness passed down from the author's parents. Their acts of giving, whether offering financial support or providing shelter to those in need, have deeply influenced Mane's understanding of community. This book encourages readers to embrace the power of giving and receiving, showing how these acts create a cycle of growth and transformation. It honors individuals who improve the world through the willingness to give, the humility to receive, and the collective effort to build a better community.

The Power of Community centers on the core principle of "giving is getting," exploring the transformative potential of giving, receiving, and growing within communities. It examines how these principles foster personal and collective development, resilience, and stronger networks. Trust, reciprocity, and leadership are vital to sustaining growth, while addressing the challenges of disconnection in modern times. Each chapter covers topics such as personal development, social change, and the importance of feedback loops. Through the *give–get–grow* framework, readers are encouraged to cultivate generosity, build connections, and contribute to thriving communities.

Contents

To my parents, whose lives of quiet generosity and selflessness have taught me that true power lies in the strength of community, the act of giving, and the growth we experience together

Preface

The Power of Community: Give, Get, and Grow is more than just a book to me—it is a reflection of the values instilled in me by my parents, the unsung heroes who taught me the true meaning of generosity and selflessness. From the earliest days of their marriage, my parents lived by the principle that giving to others is not just a responsibility but a profound privilege.

My father's actions exemplify this belief. I still marvel at the story of how, early in their marriage, he sold his engagement ring to pay for a young person's college fees. It was not a grand gesture to him but rather a natural response to someone in need. My mother, just as remarkable, supported his decisions wholeheartedly. From the very first weeks of their life together, she welcomed every guest, every soul my father brought home to help, treating each person with warmth and dignity, no matter how unexpected or challenging the circumstances.

Their home has always been a sanctuary for others—students who needed financial aid, workers seeking guidance, or even strangers needing a place to stay. Over the years, their acts of giving have taken many forms: offering financial support to someone in need, lending emotional strength during difficult times, or simply providing a listening ear. They continue to live this way, quietly yet powerfully, believing that the satisfaction and joy derived from giving and building stronger communities are rewards in themselves.

My parents' selflessness and unwavering belief in the power of community have deeply inspired me. Through their example, I've learned that giving is not merely about offering material support; it is about nurturing hope, fostering connections, and empowering others to realize their potential. They've shown me that being an unsung hero—someone who helps without the expectation of recognition—is a role of profound influence.

This book stems from their legacy and my own desire to carry forward these lessons. It is about how we, as individuals, can listen, motivate, and mentor those who just need a little support to move forward and thrive. It's a testament to the power of giving and receiving, and how these acts can create a cycle of growth—not only for those we help but for ourselves as well.

As you read these pages, I hope you find inspiration to embrace the power of community, to give with open hearts, to receive with humility, and to grow alongside others. This book is a tribute to the enduring spirit of kindness and connection that my parents have shown me and to the countless unsung heroes who quietly transform lives and build communities every single day.

May we all find the courage to give, the grace to receive, and the wisdom to grow.

Keywords

Community Building; Leadership; Volunteerism; Personal Development; Reciprocity; Trust; Culture and Resilience

CHAPTER 1

The Power of Community

Humans as Social Creatures

Giving is getting. Human beings are inherently social creatures, deeply wired for connection. From the earliest days of civilization, survival depended on cooperation and mutual support. Imagine small hunter-gatherer groups roaming vast, untamed landscapes thousands of years ago—working together to track animals, gather fruits, and construct shelters. These early societies were not random clusters of people but carefully organized networks where each individual's role contributed to the collective's survival. Hunters brought in meat to sustain the group, gatherers sought out roots and herbs for sustenance and healing, and builders created rudimentary shelters to protect against harsh elements. Such efforts weren't just practical; they fostered a profound sense of unity and shared purpose.

These small, close-knit communities thrived not solely because of their physical efforts but also because of the emotional bonds they cultivated. Around the communal fire, stories were told, wisdom was shared, and the seeds of culture were sown. Rituals, songs, and shared celebrations became more than moments of joy—they were tools for teaching values, preserving knowledge, and strengthening relationships. The concept of "us" versus "me" was paramount, ensuring that everyone contributed to and benefited from the group's efforts. It's no wonder that early humans who formed strong communities were the ones who prospered, while those who remained isolated struggled to survive.

Despite these advancements, the fundamental need for connection remained. In ancient Rome, bustling marketplaces became hubs of social interaction, where people not only traded goods but also exchanged news, ideas, and support. In medieval villages, festivals and religious gatherings offered a break from daily toil, reinforcing bonds within the community.

These connections weren't just about convenience; they addressed an intrinsic human desire to belong and to find meaning through relationships.

Fast forward to today, and this need for connection is more evident than ever, even as the ways we build and sustain communities have transformed. Physical proximity is no longer a prerequisite for forming meaningful connections. Modern technology has enabled virtual communities where people from different corners of the globe can come together over shared interests, hobbies, or causes. Online forums unite individuals who might never meet in person, from support groups for mental health to fan clubs for niche television shows. For instance, a teenager in a small town with few local peers who share their passion for astronomy can find an entire global network of like-minded enthusiasts online, providing a sense of belonging they might otherwise lack.

Yet, even with these technological advancements, physical communities remain vital. The bond of a neighborhood, where residents come together for block parties, safety initiatives, or simple acts of kindness like borrowing a cup of sugar, still holds immense power. During the COVID-19 (coronavirus disease 2019) pandemic, for example, we witnessed remarkable acts of community solidarity. In Italy, residents sang songs from their balconies to uplift each other during lockdowns, while across the world, individuals organized grocery deliveries for vulnerable neighbors or created online groups to support local businesses. These gestures of unity during a global crisis underscored a timeless truth: When humans come together, even in the face of adversity, they find strength and hope.

Ultimately, while the tools and methods of connection have evolved, the underlying need for community has remained constant. Whether it's in ancient caves or modern skyscrapers, humans have always sought out relationships that provide safety, support, and meaning. This deep-seated need underscores a universal truth: We are not meant to go through life alone. By forming and nurturing communities, we not only ensure our survival but also enrich our lives, finding joy, purpose, and growth in our shared human experience.

In a world that often seems driven by individualism and competition, the concept of community stands as a powerful reminder of our innate need for connection and cooperation. The prevailing narrative of "going it alone" or "climbing the ladder" can make success seem like a solitary pursuit. Yet countless examples from history, nature, and everyday life show us that we achieve far more when we come together. A community is where we find the strength to endure challenges, the support to grow, and the joy of shared success. It is the collective spirit of a community that amplifies individual efforts, transforming isolated victories into lasting legacies.

This strength of community isn't just evident in crises; it's also seen in moments of growth and celebration. Consider the way small business owners thrive in neighborhoods where the community rallies around them. Farmers' markets, for instance, are not just places to buy fresh produce; they are vibrant hubs where local farmers, artisans, and customers connect with each other. The simple act of choosing to buy from a local vendor supports not only that individual but the broader economy of the area. Relationships are forged over time, and the community grows stronger because people see their efforts collectively making a difference.

Community 3D: *Give–Get–Grow*

Each element plays a vital role in building a thriving group, where no one is left behind, and every individual has the opportunity to contribute and flourish.

Giving: The cornerstone of any strong community is the willingness to give. This doesn't always mean financial contributions; it can be time, skills, or even emotional support. A classic example is the tradition of barn-raising in rural American communities. When a family needed a barn, neighbors would come together to build it, often completing the project in a single day. This act of collective giving not only provided the family with a crucial structure but also reinforced bonds of trust and cooperation. Giving creates a ripple effect—it inspires others to give, fosters a culture of generosity, and strengthens the ties that hold a community together.

Getting: Equally important, though often overlooked, is the ability to get. Accepting help, guidance, or resources from others is not a sign of weakness but of interdependence—a key ingredient in any successful community. Imagine a struggling student who gets tutoring from a peer or a senior citizen benefiting from a neighbor's assistance with groceries.

These acts of *getting* help build bridges, reminding us that we all rely on one another at different points in our lives. Being open to getting also allows others the joy and fulfillment of giving, completing the cycle.

Growing: Growth is the natural outcome when giving and getting are in harmony. In a thriving community, growth happens at both the individual and collective levels. For example, consider the success of microfinance initiatives in developing countries. Organizations like Grameen Bank provide small loans to entrepreneurs, often women, enabling them to start or expand businesses. These women not only improve their own lives but also contribute to their communities by creating jobs, supporting local economies, and inspiring others. The *give–get–grow* framework is at play here: The organization gives resources, the recipients get support, and the entire community grows as a result.

This framework isn't limited to economic or material contributions; it extends to emotional and intellectual growth as well. In mentorship relationships, for instance, a mentor gives their time and expertise, the mentee gets guidance and knowledge, and both parties grow through the exchange. The mentee develops skills and confidence, while the mentor gains fresh perspectives and the satisfaction of shaping the future. Such dynamics illustrate how giving, getting, and growing are interconnected, creating a continuous cycle of improvement.

Communities that embody the *give–get–grow* philosophy become engines of transformation, capable of addressing even the most complex challenges. Look at movements for social change—whether it's the civil rights movement in the United States, the anti-apartheid struggle in South Africa, or environmental campaigns around the world. These efforts were not the work of individuals alone but of communities united by shared purpose and sustained by the cycle of giving, getting, and growing. People gave their time, energy, and resources to the cause. They got inspiration, solidarity, and strength from one another. Together, they grew into powerful forces that reshaped societies.

The beauty of the *give–get–grow* framework lies in its universality. It applies to all types of communities—families, workplaces, schools, neighborhoods, and even online networks. In a family, parents give their children love, guidance, and support; children get care and knowledge, and together, the family grows stronger. In workplaces, employees who collaborate, share ideas, and support each other create a culture of innovation and trust, benefiting the organization as a whole.

Ultimately, the power of a community is not just in what it achieves but in the spirit it fosters. It reminds us that our greatest joys, challenges, and milestones are best experienced together. When we commit to giving freely, getting graciously, and growing together, we unlock the true potential of human connection. We become part of something greater than ourselves—a living, breathing network of support, resilience, and shared purpose.

In a society that often prioritizes individual success, the *give–get–grow* framework offers a compelling alternative: a vision of a world where communities thrive because their members choose to lift one another up. By embracing this mindset, we not only enrich our own lives but also create a legacy of connection, kindness, and collective strength for generations to come.

The Need for Connection

While the modern world offers more opportunities than ever for social interaction, a paradox has emerged: Many people feel more isolated than ever. Technology, despite its incredible advantages, has inadvertently created new barriers to authentic connection. Social media platforms allow us to share updates, photos, and opinions with hundreds—even thousands—of people, yet these interactions often lack depth. We scroll through carefully curated feeds, compare our lives to others, and sometimes end up feeling more disconnected and inadequate than before.

Consider a young professional who moves to a new city for a job. While they may stay in touch with family and friends through video calls and social media, the lack of face-to-face interactions in their new environment can leave them feeling lonely. Even after joining online forums or social groups, they might struggle to build meaningful, in-person relationships. This experience isn't unique; studies have shown that frequent use of social media can correlate with higher feelings of loneliness, as digital interactions fail to replace the emotional richness of real-world connections.

The rise of individualism in society compounds this issue. From an early age, we are often taught to prioritize personal achievements over collaboration. The pressure to "succeed on your own" creates a sense of competition that can alienate us from those around us. For example, students in high-pressure academic environments might hesitate to share study materials or tips with peers, fearing it might give others an edge. In workplaces, colleagues might compete for promotions rather than supporting each other's growth. These behaviors erode trust and collaboration, weakening the sense of community we so desperately need.

In contrast, true community thrives on the principle of interdependence—the understanding that no one succeeds alone. A powerful example of this can be seen in team sports. In basketball, for instance, even the most talented player cannot win a game single-handedly. Success comes from players supporting each other, whether it's setting up the perfect pass, defending as a unit, or celebrating each other's contributions. Teams that embrace interdependence not only perform better but also build stronger bonds off the court.

Connection is not just a "nice-to-have"; it's a fundamental human need. Psychologists often refer to this as a "sense of belonging," a critical factor in mental health and well-being. Imagine a group of coworkers who form a book club. What starts as a shared interest in reading evolves into deeper friendships, where members support each other through career challenges, personal struggles, and life milestones. The group becomes a source of strength and joy, reminding its members that they are not alone.

Without connection, we lose a crucial part of what makes us human. Studies have shown that strong social bonds can improve mental health, reduce stress, and even extend life expectancy. For example, communities in "Blue Zones"—regions where people live significantly longer than average—share a common thread: strong social connections. In Okinawa, Japan, groups of lifelong friends, called *moais*, meet regularly to share food, stories, and support, creating a powerful safety net for emotional and practical needs.

Ultimately, the need for connection is universal. Whether it's a neighborhood block party, a parent–teacher association, or a group of friends gathering to share a meal, these moments of genuine interaction remind us of our shared humanity. They encourage us to support one another, celebrate each other's achievements, and find strength in the bonds we build. In these spaces, we rediscover the power of empathy, compassion, and understanding, which can heal wounds and bridge divides. When we come together, we create a foundation for resilience, allowing us to face challenges with a sense of unity and purpose that we could never achieve alone.

In a world where it's easy to feel disconnected, it's more important than ever to prioritize real, meaningful relationships. The act of coming together, whether in person or through shared experiences, fosters a sense of belonging that transcends the superficial nature of digital interactions. Connection is not just about proximity—it's about the depth and quality of the relationships we nurture. By embracing our interdependence and supporting each other, we not only create stronger communities but also enhance our own well-being. As we continue to navigate the complexities of modern life, we must remember that the most fulfilling journeys are those we take together.

The Essence of Community

At its core, a community is more than just a group of people. A community is a living organism that thrives on relationships—relationships that are built on trust, cooperation, and shared purpose. Whether it's a neighborhood, a workplace, a faith group, or an online network, communities are held together by bonds that create a sense of belonging. These bonds are the glue that not only holds the group together but propels it forward. They provide individuals with a sense of identity and security, encouraging them to contribute their unique skills and talents for the collective benefit.

But what makes a community truly powerful is the idea of collective strength. As the saying goes, "A rising tide lifts all boats." When individuals in a community thrive, the entire community benefits. This is the principle that underpins the *give–get–grow* framework: the idea that by giving to others, by receiving from others, and by growing together, a community becomes a force for good—transforming both individuals and the collective whole. This dynamic is seen in local food banks, for example, where members donate time, money, or resources to ensure that no one in the community goes hungry. In return, those who give often receive the reward of knowing they've contributed to something greater than themselves, and the community as a whole becomes stronger, more resilient, and more connected.

Consider the story of hygge (pronounced hoo-gah), a Danish cultural practice that highlights the power of community. In Denmark, where winters are long and dark, people combat isolation and harsh weather through intentional gatherings, creating cozy, warm environments where food, conversation, and togetherness thrive. This collective practice not only boosts individual happiness but also cements Denmark's reputation as one of the happiest countries in the world. Hygge underscores that communities are not just about proximity; they are about fostering emotional connections. Similarly, in countries like Japan, where the concept of *ikigai* encourages individuals to find purpose through service to others, communities are formed around the shared mission of supporting one another's well-being.

In the workplace, community is often the foundation for innovation and collaboration. Successful companies recognize the value of creating an inclusive environment where employees feel valued and supported. Whether it's through team-building exercises, mentorship programs, or simply fostering an open-door policy for communication, companies that prioritize community tend to have higher employee satisfaction and productivity. A sense of belonging within a workplace community leads to greater trust, stronger teamwork, and ultimately, better results for everyone involved.

This principle extends to every facet of society, proving that the essence of community is not just a social luxury but a vital necessity. When individuals feel connected to something greater than themselves, whether it's through shared values, goals, or experiences, they are more likely to contribute positively to the greater good. Whether it's a neighborhood working together to create a community garden or a church group organizing a volunteer outreach program, these acts of collaboration illustrate how powerful and transformative community can be in shaping our lives and the world around us.

The True Potential of Community

What sets a strong community apart is its ability to bring out the best in its members. A well-connected group doesn't just provide a sense of belonging—it actively nurtures the growth and development of each individual. A healthy community amplifies its members' strengths, compensates for their weaknesses, and creates opportunities for personal and collective growth. It fosters an environment where everyone can contribute, learn, and evolve together. This interconnectedness allows for the sharing of knowledge, skills, and resources that would be difficult, if not impossible, to access on one's own. In a true community, everyone's success is intertwined with that of others, leading to a sense of collective achievement and fulfillment. It thrives on the principle of collective strength: When individuals grow, the entire group prospers. When people support each other, they create a foundation where the group can weather challenges, overcome adversity, and build a stronger future together. This idea is encapsulated in the proverb, "If you want to go fast, go alone. If you want to go far, go together." It reminds us that true success—whether personal or collective—is built on collaboration and shared effort.

A striking example of this collective power is seen in the small Japanese island of Okinawa, known for its high concentration of centenarians. Okinawa's remarkable longevity is not a coincidence; it's a result of a deep-seated cultural practice that values social connection. One key reason for their extended lifespans is the concept of *moai*, a lifelong social support group. From childhood, Okinawans are integrated into tight-knit communities that provide emotional, financial, and practical support throughout their lives. These networks are not just about socializing—they serve as a vital safety net, ensuring that individuals have the support they need to navigate life's challenges. The members of a *moai* group hold each other accountable for their health, well-being, and life choices, which encourages healthier habits, reduces stress, and promotes a profound sense of belonging. This robust system of mutual care helps protect against the isolation that many people face in other societies, particularly as they age.

This is a testament to the transformative power of community. Through shared effort and mutual care, communities like those in Okinawa showcase how human interdependence can enhance both individual well-being and collective prosperity. By providing consistent support, encouragement, and companionship, these communities enable individuals to flourish across the entire lifespan. The fact that Okinawans not

only live longer but live healthier, more fulfilled lives speaks to the enduring strength of interconnectedness. The *moai* principle reflects the understanding that human beings are not isolated entities but part of a broader
social ecosystem where each person's well-being contributes to the health
of the whole group. Communities like those in Okinawa demonstrate
that when people come together to support one another, the benefits ripple outward, enriching everyone involved.

Beyond Okinawa, this principle can be seen in many aspects of life.
In families, neighborhoods, and workplaces, a strong sense of community promotes resilience in the face of challenges and helps individuals
maintain a sense of purpose and direction. When people work together
toward a shared goal, they are more likely to achieve it, both because of
the diverse talents they bring to the table and the collective energy they
generate. A community's true potential lies in its ability to create environments where individuals can thrive while simultaneously strengthening
the bonds that hold the group together.

The Challenge of Disconnection in Modern Times

In an era dominated by technology and constant connectivity, one would
assume that disconnection is no longer a problem. Yet, paradoxically, the
modern world is facing an increasing challenge of disconnection, not from
people, but from deeper aspects of life. As social media, messaging apps,
and instant notifications blur the lines between work and leisure, many
individuals find themselves disconnected from their own well-being, relationships, and even their sense of purpose. The relentless pace of modern
life, compounded by digital distractions, has led to a widespread sense of
isolation, despite being more "connected" than ever before.

In today's world, opportunities for connection are abundant, yet
many feel isolated. Social media, for instance, has given rise to a paradox:
We are more connected than ever, but the depth of those connections
often leaves much to be desired. Scrolling through curated images and
posts can create the illusion of connection while increasing feelings of
loneliness. We are growing toward being a community while still being
distant or alone. There is loneliness in a group, in a team or maybe sur-
rounded by people.

One of the primary ways disconnection manifests is in the decline of meaningful face-to-face interactions. While digital platforms offer an abundance of opportunities for communication, these interactions often lack the depth and emotional resonance of in-person conversations. People, especially younger generations, are now more likely to interact via text or social media posts, leading to a shallow form of connection that can leave individuals feeling lonelier and more misunderstood. The rise of virtual environments, like social media and gaming, while providing new modes of connection, often exacerbate the sense of emptiness by encouraging superficial exchanges and creating environments where individuals compare themselves to curated online personas.

An illustrative example is the phenomenon of "urban loneliness." Despite living in densely populated cities, many individuals struggle to find meaningful relationships. The pressure to succeed, the fast pace of urban life, and societal focus on self-reliance have created an environment where people hesitate to ask for help or offer support. The very fabric of community—interdependence—is often undervalued in these settings.

Ultimately, the challenge of disconnection in modern times is not just about physical or digital separation from others, but the deeper emotional, psychological, and spiritual distances that emerge in our fast-paced, technology-driven world. Finding balance and reconnecting with oneself, others, and the environment is essential for overcoming the alienating effects of modern life.

Giving Is Getting

The beauty of giving lies in its paradoxical nature: In the very act of giving, we inherently receive. This principle reflects a profound truth about human connection—when we extend kindness, share knowledge, or offer support, we create ripples of goodwill that inevitably return to us in transformative and often unexpected ways. Giving fosters trust, strengthens relationships, and nurtures a sense of purpose, all of which enrich our lives in profound and meaningful ways. Imagine the warmth that comes from sharing a meal with someone who is hungry. At that moment, the giver is not just alleviating the recipient's need; they are also building a bridge of compassion and experiencing a deep sense of fulfillment and connection that transcends the material value of the meal.

The concept of "giving is getting" reflects the idea that generosity or selflessness often leads to receiving benefits in return, whether directly or indirectly. By offering our time, resources, or support to others, we can foster goodwill, build meaningful relationships, and create a cycle of mutual support. In many cases, what we give to others ultimately returns to us in ways we might not expect. This idea is reflected in many aspects of life, from personal relationships to professional settings, and can lead to emotional fulfillment, strengthened connections, and even material rewards.

Even in small, everyday gestures, the "give is get" principle shines. Think of someone holding the door open for a stranger or offering a genuine compliment. While these actions may seem minor, they often result in a smile, a thank-you, or even a lasting positive impression that uplifts both parties. On a larger scale, movements like community service initiatives or disaster relief efforts showcase this truth powerfully. Volunteers who spend their time and energy helping others often speak of the immense satisfaction, perspective, and camaraderie they gain—an emotional and social return that no amount of money could buy.

Giving is an act of sowing seeds, and as those seeds grow, they yield fruits not just for the recipients but for the givers as well. In essence, to give is to open oneself to the abundance of connection, gratitude, and growth, making the act of giving an intrinsic form of receiving. This profound interplay underscores that our contributions to others are not just isolated acts but investments in a collective well-being that uplifts and transforms us all.

In relationships, the idea of "giving is getting" is also evident. When you listen to a friend's problems and offer emotional support during a tough time, you are giving something valuable—your time, empathy, and care. In return, when you go through your own difficulties, your friend is more likely to reciprocate, offering you the same support in your time of need. This reciprocity deepens the relationship, strengthening the bond between you. Similarly, by lending resources, such as tools to a neighbor for a home improvement project, you contribute to a sense of community and cooperation. Over time, these acts of kindness can lead to your neighbor returning the favor, whether by helping with your own projects or offering assistance in some other way.

From a philosophical perspective, the principle of "giving is getting" aligns with teachings found in many spiritual and cultural traditions. In Buddhism, for instance, the act of giving (or *dāna*) is viewed as a way to accumulate positive karma, which in turn brings blessings back to the giver. Similarly, in Hinduism, the law of karma suggests that good actions lead to good outcomes. By contributing to the well-being of others, we align ourselves with forces of compassion and positivity, which eventually circle back to us.

Ultimately, the idea of "giving is getting" is a powerful reminder that generosity, kindness, and selflessness not only improve the lives of others but also enrich our own. Whether through emotional satisfaction, strengthened relationships, or even material returns, the act of giving creates a cycle of positivity that benefits both the giver and the recipient. By investing in others through our time, energy, and resources, we often find that what we give comes back to us in ways that help us grow and thrive.

While the act of giving is vital, it is equally important to recognize that receiving is an essential part of the cycle. Giving without ever allowing oneself to receive can lead to burnout or feelings of being undervalued. There is a natural balance between the two, and at some point, everyone will find themselves in a position where they need help, support, or kindness. Being open to receiving is not only a way to restore one's energy and spirit but also a way to acknowledge the interconnectedness of human relationships. When we allow ourselves to receive, we create opportunities for others to give, which in turn strengthens the bonds between us. It's important to remember that receiving is not a sign of weakness but an integral part of a healthy, reciprocal dynamic where both individuals can thrive. Just as we benefit from giving, we also enrich our lives when we accept the generosity of others, fostering a cycle of mutual care and support.

The Ripple Effect of Giving and Getting

The ripple effect of giving and getting is a powerful phenomenon that illustrates how small acts of generosity can create far-reaching impacts, often in ways that are not immediately visible. Just like the way a stone creates ripples when dropped into water, one act of kindness or support can expand outward, influencing not only the immediate recipient but also many others in unexpected ways. This cycle of giving and receiving fosters a sense of interconnectedness and community, where the actions of individuals have the potential to create a lasting, positive impact on a larger scale.

One real-world example of the ripple effect can be seen in charitable giving. Consider a person who donates a significant sum of money to a local homeless shelter. While the immediate effect is that the shelter can provide more services to individuals in need, the long-term ripple effect is even more profound. The people who benefit from the shelter may receive not only food and shelter but also counseling, job training, and the chance to reintegrate into society. Some of these individuals, once they regain stability, might go on to volunteer at the shelter, donate money, or help others in their community. Over time, these positive actions can lead to a decrease in homelessness and a stronger, more supportive community, demonstrating how one act of giving can multiply its effects.

The ripple effect is also apparent in everyday acts of kindness. A person who helps a stranger by holding the door open or offering directions might brighten their day and create a moment of connection. This small, seemingly insignificant gesture might inspire the recipient to perform a similar act of kindness toward someone else, thereby spreading positive energy throughout the community. Over time, these small actions accumulate and create a more compassionate society. A study conducted in 2008 by psychologist Nicholas Christakis and sociologist James Fowler found that acts of kindness and generosity could spread through social networks, influencing not only the direct recipients but also people in their extended networks, showing just how interconnected our actions truly are.

Even on a global scale, the ripple effect of giving and receiving can lead to widespread social change. The actions of organizations like the Bill and Melinda Gates Foundation or groups like Doctors Without Borders are prime examples. Through their charitable work and humanitarian efforts, they provide vital resources, medical care, and education to underserved populations around the world. While these organizations give to those in need, the recipients of their aid often go on to contribute in their own ways—whether by returning to their communities to help others or by creating local initiatives that tackle the same issues. These ripples of giving and receiving can ultimately lead to a shift in global attitudes toward social responsibility, with people becoming more inclined to contribute to causes greater than themselves.

In all these examples, the ripple effect shows how giving and receiving can snowball into something much larger than the initial act. By giving to others, we not only provide immediate benefits but also sow the seeds for future generosity, support, and growth. And when we are open to receiving, we allow others the opportunity to participate in this cycle, reinforcing the interconnectedness of our actions. Ultimately, the ripple effect of giving and receiving creates a continuous flow of kindness, support, and positive change that can resonate through entire communities and even the world.

Growth Through Connection

Growth through connection is a profound concept that highlights the power of relationships, collaboration, and shared experiences in fostering personal, professional, and collective growth. It emphasizes that human beings do not develop in isolation but rather through the connections they make with others. These connections can take many forms—whether they be familial, friendships, professional networks, or community ties— but all contribute to the evolution of an individual. By building meaningful connections, people gain access to new perspectives, resources, and support systems, all of which are critical for personal and communal development.

One of the most powerful ways growth occurs through connection is within personal relationships. Consider the impact of a supportive friendship. A person who feels isolated may struggle with personal challenges, such as stress, self-doubt, or career uncertainty. However, by building a connection with a friend who offers understanding, encouragement, and advice, that individual can gain a fresh perspective on their challenges. This connection provides emotional support, a sense of belonging, and the confidence to take action toward overcoming obstacles. For example, a person who has been struggling to make a career change might find new motivation and insight by confiding in a friend who has gone through a similar experience. The emotional support and shared experience of their friendship can empower them to take the next step, ultimately leading to personal growth and success.

Professional networks also exemplify how growth occurs through connection. In the workplace, connections often lead to learning, new opportunities, and career advancement. A young professional might struggle to navigate the complexities of a new industry, but by forming relationships with experienced colleagues or mentors, they can accelerate their learning and gain valuable insights. A mentor might provide guidance on strategic decision making, offer career advice, or introduce the mentee to important contacts in the field. This connection doesn't just benefit the mentee—it also contributes to the mentor's growth, as they strengthen their leadership and coaching skills. In this way, professional connections foster a cycle of mutual growth. For example, a recent college graduate working at a tech company may feel uncertain about their role, but by connecting with a senior developer who offers advice on coding best practices and career development, they may quickly become more confident and capable, paving the way for career advancement.

Furthermore, community connections often spark collective growth, where individuals unite to achieve common goals. A strong sense of community fosters collaboration, resource-sharing, and collective problem-solving. Consider the example of a community coming together to address a local environmental issue, such as pollution or access to clean water. By connecting with others who share similar concerns, individuals can pool resources, exchange ideas, and organize efforts that lead to impactful change. This collaboration leads to growth on both an individual and collective level. People may learn new skills—such as organizing events, campaigning for change, or even technical skills like water purification. At the same time, the community as a whole grows stronger and more resilient, as it becomes better equipped to address future challenges. For instance, a group of citizens who unite to clean up a local park might not only improve their environment but also develop a deeper sense of community, gain new friendships, and inspire others to take action.

In the realm of education and mentorship, growth through connection is particularly evident. Teachers and students experience growth through their interactions, but so too do peers who work together to learn. For example, a student struggling with mathematics might form a study group with classmates, where each member brings their unique strengths to the table. One student may have a talent for explaining complex concepts, while another excels at applying them in real-world scenarios. By working together, they deepen their understanding of the subject and improve their individual skills. These peer connections can also motivate students to push beyond their limits, encouraging each other to succeed. The sense of collaboration and shared achievement in such study groups can lead to enhanced academic growth and self-confidence.

Ultimately, growth through connection shows that human beings are inherently social creatures who thrive when they come together. Whether through personal relationships, professional networks, community engagement, or even intellectual collaboration, the connections we make are the fertile soil from which growth can spring. These connections allow us to gain new perspectives, share knowledge, and develop the emotional and intellectual tools we need to navigate life's challenges. By recognizing the importance of our connections with others and fostering meaningful relationships, we can unlock our full potential and continue to grow in ways we might never have imagined on our own.

Give–Get–Grow Framework

The true potential of a community is realized only when its members are committed to giving, getting, and growing together. This is the foundation of the *give–get–grow* framework—a dynamic cycle that fosters healthier, more connected communities. In the context of the *give–get–grow* framework, growth becomes the natural outcome of the dynamic interplay between giving and receiving. This framework emphasizes that by giving—whether it's our time, resources, or support—we create opportunities for others, and in turn, we open ourselves up to receiving in return, whether through tangible rewards or intangible benefits like knowledge, connections, and emotional fulfillment. The act of giving lays the foundation for growth, while receiving nurtures and sustains it. When both elements are in balance, they fuel each other, creating a continuous cycle of improvement and progress.

The *give–get–grow* framework works in such a way that giving helps us cultivate positive relationships, expand our horizons, and contribute to the well-being of others. By doing so, we often find ourselves enriched in ways we might not have anticipated. As we receive in return—whether it's through learning, support, or new opportunities—our capacity for growth expands. This reciprocal process enables us to evolve, both personally and professionally. For example, by giving mentorship to someone, we not only help them grow but also learn from the experience, which in turn strengthens our own skills and perspectives.

In essence, growth is both the reward and the catalyst in this framework. Through the process of giving and receiving, we unlock potential—both within ourselves and in others—leading to mutual development. As we grow, we become more capable of giving, which continues the cycle. This ongoing loop of giving, getting, and growing forms the foundation of thriving communities, prosperous careers, and enriched lives, demonstrating that growth is not just a personal endeavor but a collective journey nurtured by the connections we make and the contributions we offer.

The Role of Shared Purpose

Shared purpose is a powerful driver of growth, collaboration, and meaningful connections. When individuals or groups come together around a common goal, they are more likely to experience deeper engagement, a stronger sense of belonging, and enhanced performance. A shared purpose aligns the efforts of diverse people, creating a unified sense of direction that can overcome challenges and foster innovation. Whether in personal relationships, professional teams, or larger societal movements, shared purpose acts as a binding force that propels individuals to not only achieve their goals but also grow and learn from the experience.

One of the clearest examples of shared purpose can be seen in workplace teams. Consider a company facing a major product launch. Employees from different departments—marketing, design, engineering, and customer support—come together with a shared purpose: to successfully launch a product that meets customer needs and drives company growth. Each department brings its unique expertise, but their efforts are aligned toward one common goal. This shared purpose fosters collaboration and reduces friction, as individuals understand that their success is dependent on the success of the group. For instance, the marketing team might craft the campaign around the product's features, while the engineering team ensures the product functions flawlessly, and the customer support team prepares to address any issues that arise. When the product is finally launched and succeeds, the shared purpose not only leads to business success but also to a stronger sense of accomplishment and connection among the employees, reinforcing teamwork and inspiring further innovation.

In nonprofit organizations or social movements, shared purpose can be a powerful motivator that drives individuals to contribute their time, energy, and resources. Take, for example, organizations like Doctors Without Borders or environmental groups like 350.org. Volunteers and employees within these organizations are united by the shared purpose of improving global health or addressing climate change. This sense of purpose provides a sense of meaning that transcends individual roles and personal gain, motivating people to work long hours, travel to difficult or dangerous locations, and often put their personal lives on hold for the greater good. For instance, a doctor volunteering in a war-torn region with Doctors Without Borders may work under challenging conditions, but the shared purpose of providing critical health care to underserved populations gives them a sense of fulfillment and drives them to persevere. This shared sense of mission not only impacts the individuals involved but also creates a ripple effect, inspiring others to join the cause or support the movement in various ways.

Shared purpose is also a cornerstone of educational and mentoring relationships. Consider a mentor and mentee working together on a specific professional goal, such as writing a book, building a career, or launching a project. The mentor shares their expertise, and the mentee brings their ideas, ambitions, and challenges to the table. The shared purpose of accomplishing a specific goal—such as publishing a book or succeeding in a particular career path—aligns their efforts, creating a productive and rewarding relationship. The mentor gains satisfaction from guiding someone through the process, while the mentee experiences growth from the mentor's guidance. This shared purpose leads to both individuals learning and evolving. Over time, the mentee may become a mentor themselves, passing on the lessons learned, creating a cycle of growth that continues with each new connection.

In sports teams, shared purpose is foundational to team success. When athletes come together for a common goal, such as winning a championship or improving performance, the sense of purpose drives not only their physical preparation but also their mental and emotional resilience. For instance, a football team working toward a playoff appearance must coordinate their efforts on and off the field, with each player understanding how their individual role contributes to the larger objective. The shared purpose unites them in the face of setbacks and motivates them through tough training sessions. This unity is often reflected in the team's culture and dynamics, with players supporting each other and pushing one another to be better. The collective effort of achieving a shared goal deepens their commitment to one another and to the mission of the team, contributing to both individual and group growth.

In conclusion, the role of shared purpose in growth is undeniable. Whether in personal relationships, professional settings, social movements, or global initiatives, a shared sense of mission aligns efforts, strengthens bonds, and drives individuals and groups to reach their full potential. The power of shared purpose is transformative, as it fosters collaboration, innovation, and growth. When people come together for a common cause, they create not only stronger connections but also opportunities for mutual growth and meaningful success.

The *give–get–grow* framework offers a timeless and powerful model for creating positive change and fostering personal, professional, and communal growth. As we look toward the future, the core principles of giving, receiving, and growing will continue to be essential in navigating an increasingly interconnected and dynamic world. In a time when challenges like climate change, economic disparity, and societal fragmentation are growing, the *give–get–grow* framework can serve as a guiding light, helping individuals, organizations, and communities not only survive but thrive through collaboration and mutual support.

Looking forward, we can see a future where the *give–get–grow* framework acts as a cornerstone for sustainable development, innovation, and human connection. In the realm of social responsibility, companies and organizations will increasingly adopt models that balance profit with positive societal impact. For example, companies like Patagonia and Ben & Jerry's have demonstrated the power of integrating giving into their business practices by supporting environmental causes, promoting fair labor practices, and championing social justice issues. These companies give to the community by supporting causes they care about, get returns in the form of customer loyalty, and grow by fostering a culture of ethical responsibility that attracts both talent and consumers. The more organizations and businesses adopt this framework, the more they will contribute to a global economy that values people over profits and purpose over short-term gains.

On a personal level, individuals who embrace the *give–get–grow* framework will cultivate stronger relationships, enhance their own personal development, and become more empathetic global citizens. Imagine the impact of someone giving their time to mentor a young person. The mentor gives advice, shares experiences, and helps the mentee navigate challenges, yet the mentor also grows by learning through the process. They might gain new insights, discover new perspectives, or be inspired to continue their own growth journey. The mentee, in turn, benefits from guidance and emotional support, and as they grow, they may, in turn, mentor someone else, perpetuating the cycle of growth. This process demonstrates how giving and receiving create a powerful dynamic of growth, where both individuals evolve in ways they could not have imagined on their own.

The role of shared purpose in the *give–get–grow* framework is central to fostering unity and collective progress. We are already witnessing the power of shared purpose in addressing global challenges. Initiatives like The Paris Agreement on climate change, which brings together world leaders, organizations, and activists to address environmental issues, are powerful examples of how shared purpose leads to transformative growth. As countries, corporations, and individuals unite under common goals like sustainability, equality, and justice, the potential for meaningful change is immense. Through these collaborations, we witness that giving resources, support, and time to a cause ultimately leads to growth—not only for the cause itself but for the individuals and communities involved.

Looking ahead, the *give–get–grow* framework has the potential to transform global systems, creating more equitable, compassionate, and resilient societies. From corporate social responsibility (CSR) to community-driven change and personal development, the principles of giving, receiving, and growing will create a future where individuals and organizations thrive by helping each other. As we face complex, interconnected global challenges, the framework offers a solution rooted in human connection and mutual support—showing that in a world of rapid change, collaboration and generosity are the keys to sustainable growth.

The vision for the future is one in which we continue to build upon the foundational principles of the *give–get–grow* framework—where each act of giving creates a wave of growth that benefits both the giver and the receiver. As we move forward, this cycle of giving, receiving, and growing will not only enrich our personal and professional lives but will also serve as a blueprint for creating a more compassionate, innovative, and interconnected world.

CHAPTER 2

The Principle of Giving

Giving is an act that transcends culture, geography, and time. It is as old as humanity itself, woven into the fabric of every culture, every society, and has remained a cornerstone of human interaction across centuries. From the early days of human existence, when tribes and communities shared food, shelter, and resources to ensure collective survival, to the modern-day acts of philanthropy and charitable giving, the principle of giving has been a fundamental part of how we relate to one another. In many ancient societies, the concept of "sharing" was essential for survival; it was not only about physical resources but also about ensuring social cohesion and mutual support. Whether it was the communal feasts of indigenous tribes or the practices of ancient civilizations where offerings were made to gods or shared with the less fortunate, giving was a core part of human life. This idea of giving, which often arose from necessity, evolved over time into more formalized practices of charity, social welfare, and philanthropy that we see today.

Despite this long history, in the modern world—where individualism and self-interest often dominate many aspects of life—the act of giving remains one of the most powerful forces for creating meaningful, lasting change. In a society driven by consumerism, personal success, and material wealth, giving continues to be an enduring reminder of what truly matters: human connection, empathy, and shared responsibility. Selfless giving is not merely a gesture of kindness but a transformative act that strengthens bonds, promotes social justice, and encourages a deeper sense of purpose in individuals and communities. From small acts of kindness, like offering help to a neighbor in need, to grand-scale acts of generosity, such as significant charitable donations to global causes, the principle of giving has the ability to shape lives, uplift others, and create positive ripple effects far beyond the immediate moment.

What is truly remarkable about giving is its universality. While the forms of giving may differ—whether in the form of donations, volunteerism, or the simple act of lending a helping hand—its core value remains constant across the globe. It is an expression of humanity's shared values and the recognition that we are all connected. In cultures across the world, giving is seen not only as a duty but as a means of personal and collective growth. In many indigenous cultures, for instance, the act of giving is tied to reciprocity, where what one person offers is returned in different forms, creating a cycle of mutual support and growth. Even in the most challenging circumstances, people find ways to give, whether it is through time, talent, or resources. In this way, giving transcends material wealth or social status, reminding us that true generosity is not just about what we have, but about the willingness to share with others.

As the world continues to face complex challenges—from climate change and poverty to political instability and inequality—the principle of giving offers a powerful antidote to division and hardship. When communities come together to share resources, knowledge, and compassion, they create a more resilient and harmonious world. In a time when individualistic pursuits often take precedence, the act of giving serves as a reminder of the importance of interdependence and community. In this way, giving is not just about what we give, but about the deeper connections it fosters, the growth it nurtures, and the lasting impact it leaves on the world.

The Heart of Giving

This simple yet powerful concept is a deeply rooted concept that extends far beyond the transactional nature of charity. It is the embodiment of empathy, compassion, and the willingness to uplift others, often at the expense of one's own comfort. This act of selflessness can take many forms, from the simple gesture of a neighbor helping with groceries to large-scale humanitarian efforts that require immense personal sacrifice. At its core, the *heart of giving* is driven by the understanding that there is a collective responsibility to support one another, and that our individual actions, no matter how small, can create a larger impact in the lives of others.

Similarly, community-driven acts of giving are also examples of how the heart of giving functions on a local level. In times of crisis, like during the COVID-19 pandemic, people showed up for each other in remarkable ways. From volunteers delivering groceries to the elderly to people sewing face masks for health care workers, these acts of kindness were not only about helping others but about creating a sense of solidarity in the face of adversity. The *Heart of Giving* thrives in moments when people set aside their own needs and respond to the suffering or needs of others with empathy and action. It's the recognition that we are interconnected, and in giving, we enrich not only others but ourselves, creating a cycle of generosity that ultimately strengthens the fabric of society.

Through both personal and global examples, it's clear that the *heart of giving* isn't just about charity—it's about fostering human connection, igniting social change, and ensuring that compassion is at the center of all our interactions. Whether through a simple gesture or large-scale social movements, the essence of giving lies in the intention to make the world a more compassionate place, reminding us that even the smallest act of kindness has the potential to transform lives.

At its core, giving is about sharing what we have—whether it's our time, our resources, our knowledge, or even our love—with others. It's a simple, yet profound, act of generosity that says, "I have enough to share, and I want to help you." But the act of giving is more than just a gesture; it is a mindset, an expression of abundance. When we give, we signal to ourselves and to others that we believe in the value of connection, that we are part of something larger than ourselves.

The *heart of giving* ties seamlessly into the *give–get–grow* framework by demonstrating how acts of generosity and selflessness lead to personal and collective transformation. The *give–get–grow* framework operates on the principle that giving creates a cycle where individuals not only contribute to the well-being of others but also receive growth, fulfillment, and success in return. The *heart of giving* is a core catalyst for initiating this cycle.

The *get* phase of the framework highlights that even though the primary intention in giving is not to receive, giving often leads to unexpected returns. These can be material, emotional, or spiritual rewards. For instance, someone who donates to a cause may experience a sense of fulfillment, knowing they've made a tangible difference. Similarly, those who volunteer in community projects might form deeper relationships and build stronger connections with others. This reciprocal benefit is not always tangible but often manifests as a sense of purpose, personal growth, and an enhanced understanding of others' needs.

As individuals engage in the act of giving, they naturally grow. Whether it's gaining new skills, expanding one's empathy, or developing leadership capabilities, the process of giving fosters personal development. For example, a mentor who gives their time to guide a younger individual not only impacts their mentee's life but also refines their own communication and leadership skills. This personal growth can lead to increased professional and social opportunities, expanding one's influence and ability to contribute to society. The *heart of giving* here reflects the growth of an individual's character and the community's collective well-being. As people continue to give, they grow in their capacity to make a positive difference, resulting in a more generous and compassionate society.

In this way, the *heart of giving* directly ties to the *give–get–grow* framework by showing that generosity fosters a cycle of growth. By giving without expecting immediate returns, individuals often find that they "get" in terms of personal rewards or a sense of fulfillment, which leads to further growth in their abilities, perspectives, and influence. This growth then enables them to give even more, creating a continuous *loop of positive impact.*

Giving Beyond Material Resources

A powerful expression of generosity that transcends the typical notion of charity, which often focuses on financial or material donations. True giving encompasses emotional, intellectual, and social resources that can have an equally, if not more, profound impact on others. This kind of giving demonstrates that generosity is not limited to what can be bought or measured but is also about offering intangible qualities like time, attention, empathy, knowledge, and care.

Additionally, acts of emotional support, such as listening or offering a kind word, can have a profound effect on someone's well-being. For example, a teacher who spends extra time after class helping struggling students with personal problems, or a friend who listens attentively during a difficult time, offers more than just a friendly ear—they give their emotional presence, which can be life-changing. Studies have shown that social and emotional connections are just as critical to mental health as physical resources, and these types of nonmaterial gifts can deeply enhance one's sense of belonging and self-worth.

Lastly, *giving beyond material resources* can be seen in the countless individuals who volunteer their time in disaster relief efforts. In these critical moments, what people offer is not money, but their labor, skills, and emotional stamina. For example, during the aftermath of natural disasters like hurricanes or earthquakes, volunteers often arrive on the scene to provide not only physical labor but also emotional support to victims who may have lost everything. These volunteers offer comfort and a sense of hope, helping others rebuild their lives in ways that go far beyond tangible items.

In all of these examples, giving beyond material resources demonstrates that the most powerful gifts are often those that can't be purchased or quantified. Emotional support, time, knowledge, and a willingness to listen or act all create lasting impacts that go beyond the immediate. These intangible resources are often more enduring than material things, as they have the power to heal, inspire, and change lives in ways money alone cannot.

The Chain Reaction of Giving

The *chain reaction of giving* refers to the idea that acts of generosity, no matter how small, can create a cascade of positive outcomes that spread far beyond the original act. When a person gives, whether through time, resources, or emotional support, the benefits often extend to others in unexpected ways. This chain reaction can inspire others to give, create lasting changes in communities, and even influence societal norms, leading to a more compassionate and interconnected world.

One real-world example of the *chain reaction of giving* can be seen in the *Pay It Forward* movement. This concept gained popularity in the early 2000s and involves doing something kind for someone without expecting anything in return, with the hope that the recipient will pass on the kindness to someone else. A simple act, like paying for a stranger's coffee, can inspire that person to perform a good deed for another, creating a continuous cycle of generosity. In some cases, people have paid for a stranger's groceries, offered help to those in need, or volunteered their time, all as part of a larger movement of giving that has a chain reaction across communities. The chain of kindness often spreads well beyond the initial act, as people carry the spirit of generosity forward in their daily lives.

Another powerful example is seen in disaster relief efforts. When a natural disaster strikes, such as a hurricane, earthquake, or wildfire, communities often come together to provide aid. But the chain reaction doesn't stop there. After a major event, volunteers who have participated in relief efforts often feel inspired to engage in future charitable activities, while donors who have given money or supplies continue to support causes related to the disaster long after the immediate need has passed. The widespread media coverage of these acts of kindness can also inspire others around the world to contribute in some way, whether by sending money, raising nto their business practices, or creating a broader shift in how companies view profit and purpose.

Another profound example of the chain reaction of giving comes from *community-based volunteer work*. Consider organizations like *Habitat for Humanity*, which involves volunteers in building homes for families in need. The volunteers who participate in these projects often gain a deep sense of fulfillment, which motivates them to continue giving, whether through additional volunteering or by supporting other charitable causes. This act of giving also influences the lives of the recipients, who often become empowered to pay it forward in their own communities by helping others, thereby continuing the cycle of generosity.

Ultimately, the *chain reaction of giving* highlights how a single act of kindness or generosity can expand and multiply, creating a broader impact that benefits not just the recipient, but also the giver, their community, and society at large. It is a powerful reminder that even the smallest gestures, when done with genuine care and intent, can set off a chain reaction of goodwill that continues to spread far and wide.

Overcoming the Fear of Giving

Despite the inherent power of giving, many people hesitate. They worry they don't have enough to give, that their contribution won't make a difference, or that they will be taken advantage of. These fears can stem from a mindset of scarcity—the belief that there is not enough to go around and that if we give too much, we might be left with nothing.

However, the principle of giving is rooted in abundance. It's about the belief that there is always enough to share. The more we give, the more we open ourselves to receive—not just in material terms, but in the form of emotional and spiritual growth, connection, and fulfillment. Giving, when done from a place of generosity rather than obligation, enriches both the giver and the receiver. The real gift of giving lies not in the material exchange but in the deep sense of fulfillment and joy that comes from knowing we've made a difference in someone's life.

Overcoming the fear of giving is an important step in fostering a more generous and compassionate world. Many people hesitate when it comes to giving, whether due to concerns about their financial security, the fear of being taken advantage of, or doubts about the impact of their contributions. However, overcoming these fears can lead to profound personal and collective benefits. When individuals choose to give without fear, they often find that the rewards—both for the giver and for the recipient—far exceed any perceived risks.

A key aspect of overcoming the fear of giving is shifting the focus away from material concerns and toward the broader, long-term impact of generosity. For instance, some may worry that their contributions, whether financial, emotional, or in terms of time, are too small to make a meaningful difference. Yet even the smallest gestures can have far-reaching consequences. A single donation may seem insignificant, but when combined with others, it can lead to significant change. For example, small donations to humanitarian causes can collectively fund large-scale relief efforts, while an individual act of kindness can inspire others to give, creating a ripple effect that spreads throughout communities.

Additionally, many people fear giving because they are uncertain about the tangible effects of their contributions. They might wonder whether their efforts will truly make a difference or whether they are part of a larger effort that will have a significant impact. While it's difficult to measure the impact of every act of giving, countless examples show that even small acts of generosity can lead to far-reaching changes. When people overcome this fear and take action anyway, they often find that their contributions, no matter how small, are part of a larger, meaningful shift. Whether it's a donation to an environmental cause, volunteering at a local shelter, or supporting a social justice movement, giving is often a vital component in the larger fabric of change.

Overcoming the fear of giving can also lead to personal growth and transformation. By letting go of anxieties and doubts, individuals can experience the joy of giving, which in turn can lead to greater emotional well-being and a sense of community. Research has shown that acts of kindness and generosity can trigger the release of endorphins, fostering a sense of happiness and fulfillment. Furthermore, by giving, individuals often gain a deeper understanding of their own values and purpose, which can enrich their lives in ways that go beyond material wealth. Largely, overcoming the fear of giving involves shifting from a scarcity mindset to one of abundance. It requires trusting that our contributions—whether big or small—are meaningful and valuable, and that by giving, we make the world a better place for everyone.

In conclusion, overcoming the fear of giving is about letting go of the limitations we place on ourselves and embracing the act of generosity as a powerful tool for personal and societal transformation. The fear that holds us back—whether related to material concerns, trust, or doubts about impact—can be overcome by shifting our focus to the greater good and the long-term benefits of giving. Once we take that first step in overcoming these fears, we begin to unlock the true power of generosity, creating a world where kindness, empathy, and selflessness thrive.

Giving as a Path to Personal Growth

Giving as a path to personal growth is a concept rooted in the idea that generosity not only benefits others but also contributes significantly to the growth and development of the giver. When people give, whether through time, resources, or emotional support, they often experience a deep sense of fulfillment, self-discovery, and personal transformation. Giving allows individuals to step outside of themselves, broaden their perspectives, and cultivate qualities such as empathy, gratitude, and resilience. By giving a regular practice, individuals can create a positive feedback loop of growth that enhances their overall well-being.

One of the key ways giving promotes personal growth is by fostering empathy. When we give, especially in ways that require us to connect with others on an emotional or personal level, we develop a deeper understanding of their experiences and challenges. For example, volunteering at a local shelter can expose individuals to the struggles of those less fortunate, helping them develop a sense of empathy for people in difficult circumstances. This emotional connection can encourage the giver to adopt a more compassionate and open-minded outlook in all areas of life.

Giving also teaches resilience. Often, acts of generosity require stepping out of one's comfort zone, whether it's donating time to a cause that requires significant effort or offering emotional support to someone in crisis. These experiences can strengthen personal resilience, helping individuals develop the ability to cope with challenges and adversity. For example, someone who consistently volunteers with a youth mentorship program may face difficult moments, such as helping a young person navigate tough life situations. These experiences teach patience and adaptability, helping the giver become more resilient in the face of their own struggles.

Another powerful aspect of giving is how it can create a sense of purpose. When people contribute to causes that align with their values and passions, they often feel more connected to a larger mission. This sense of purpose can provide direction and motivation, driving individuals to grow in ways they might not have anticipated. For example, a person who starts volunteering at a local food bank may discover a passion for working in food security or social justice. This realization could lead them to pursue new career paths or educational opportunities, all because their giving experience ignited a deeper sense of purpose.

Finally, giving allows individuals to develop a sense of fulfillment that is often absent from material pursuits. Many people who experience deep personal growth through giving report feeling a sense of joy and satisfaction that goes beyond what they can acquire or achieve in traditional ways. Whether it's the fulfillment of mentoring a child, the joy of giving a meaningful gift, or the satisfaction of helping a community, giving offers an intrinsic reward that can enhance one's sense of purpose and well-being.

In conclusion, giving is more than just an act of kindness—it is a powerful tool for personal growth. Whether through the development of empathy, the cultivation of gratitude, the strengthening of resilience, the discovery of purpose, the building of relationships, or the fulfillment of meaningful goals, giving opens doors to new experiences and self-discovery. By embracing giving as a path to personal growth, individuals can enrich their own lives while positively impacting the lives of others.

The Balance of Giving and Receiving

The *balance of giving and receiving* is a vital concept in building healthy, sustainable relationships and maintaining personal well-being. While giving is often celebrated for its positive impact on others and oneself, receiving is equally important in creating a cycle of mutual respect, growth, and connection. Striking the right balance between giving and receiving ensures that generosity does not lead to burnout or feelings of inadequacy, and that receiving does not foster dependence or entitlement. Instead, it creates a harmonious flow of support, where both parties can contribute to one another's growth and happiness.

One of the finest examples of the balance between giving and receiving can be seen in the *mentor–mentee* relationship. In such relationships, the mentor gives guidance, wisdom, and support, while the mentee receives knowledge and encouragement. However, the relationship often evolves into a reciprocal one. The mentor learns from the mentee's fresh perspectives, enthusiasm, and new ideas. This balance of giving and receiving enhances both parties' growth. For example, a senior professional who mentors a younger colleague might offer career advice and share industry experience, but in turn, the mentor may gain new insights from the mentee's innovative thinking or technological skills. This reciprocal exchange enriches both individuals, helping them evolve in ways they wouldn't have on their own.

Similarly, in family dynamics, the balance of giving and receiving plays a crucial role in fostering healthy, supportive relationships. Parents, for instance, invest their time, energy, and resources in raising their children, giving love and guidance. However, as children grow, they start to give back, not just materially but emotionally. As adults, children may offer support to aging parents, assist them in daily tasks, or simply provide companionship. This ongoing cycle of giving and receiving strengthens the bond between parents and children, creating a foundation of mutual respect and care that evolves over a lifetime.

The concept is also evident in the world of charitable giving, where donors give to causes they care about, and in return, they receive a sense of fulfillment, purpose, and connection. However, it's important that charitable organizations maintain this balance. For example, when donors contribute to a nonprofit, the organization not only benefits from the resources but can offer the donor opportunities for personal growth—whether through volunteer work, networking, or a deeper understanding of social issues. The donors are often transformed by the experience of giving, learning more about the causes they support and the communities they help. In turn, the nonprofit receives the necessary resources to continue its mission, and the donor receives a sense of accomplishment, knowing they have made a difference.

A strong example of the balance of giving and receiving can be seen in the practice of *reciprocal altruism*, a concept in social psychology that explains how individuals may give to others in ways that ultimately benefit themselves as well. This might seem counterintuitive, but in practice, reciprocal giving fosters a sense of community and interdependence. In professional settings, for example, colleagues often collaborate by giving their expertise and knowledge to one another. While this might initially seem like a one-way exchange, the collective giving benefits everyone in the group—leading to stronger working relationships, greater innovation, and a more supportive environment for all. In such environments, the exchange of ideas and support creates a positive cycle of growth, making the workplace more productive and harmonious.

Ultimately, the balance of giving and receiving is not about keeping score or seeking equal exchanges at all times but rather about understanding that both elements are necessary for a thriving, fulfilling life. By recognizing when we need to give and when we need to receive, we foster healthier relationships, greater personal well-being, and a more connected community. When we embrace the ebb and flow of giving and receiving, we create a dynamic and sustainable way of interacting with the world that nurtures both others and ourselves.

The Power of Generosity

The power of generosity is a transformative force that transcends individual acts of kindness, creating widespread positive change within communities and society at large. Generosity, in its many forms—whether through time, resources, support, or emotional care—has the ability to shift not only the lives of those who receive but also the hearts and minds of those who give. When generosity is practiced consistently, it creates a ripple effect, amplifying goodwill and fostering a culture of mutual support, compassion, and interconnectedness.

One of the most profound examples of the power of generosity can be seen in the realm of community-based initiatives. When people come together to address local challenges, such as homelessness, food insecurity, or access to education, their collective generosity can completely transform a neighborhood or even an entire city. For instance, when community members volunteer their time to rebuild homes after a natural disaster or organize local food drives for those in need, they not only provide immediate relief but also strengthen the social fabric of their communities. The act of giving—whether through offering physical help, donating money, or simply showing up to support others—creates a sense of unity and shared responsibility that goes far beyond individual efforts.

In workplaces, generosity can be equally powerful. Companies that foster a culture of giving, where employees support one another and contribute to the larger mission of the organization, often see increased collaboration, higher morale, and greater overall productivity. A generous workplace is one where individuals share knowledge, lend a helping hand, and mentor each other, understanding that their collective success depends on lifting others up. In such environments, the spirit of generosity extends beyond formal charity or donations—it becomes an integral part of the day-to-day interactions, creating a positive atmosphere where everyone thrives.

Generosity also plays a transformative role in personal growth. Giving provides individuals with a sense of purpose, as they often realize the impact they can have on others' lives. The act of helping or supporting others can inspire gratitude, humility, and a deeper understanding of one's own privileges and challenges. This growth is not only internal but can also extend outward, motivating others to adopt similar attitudes of generosity. As individuals experience the joy and fulfillment that comes with giving, they often find themselves becoming more compassionate, more connected to others, and more resilient in the face of their own difficulties.

Finally, the power of generosity extends to its ability to create long-lasting societal change. When individuals and communities choose to act generously, they can influence broader systems, such as education, health care, and social justice. For example, when large groups of people come together to support causes like environmental sustainability or social equality, their collective generosity can drive significant policy changes and shift societal norms. Through sustained acts of giving—whether through advocacy, donations, or community engagement—people can create a world that is more just, equitable, and compassionate.

In conclusion, *the power of generosity* lies in its ability to create profound change on multiple levels. Whether it's the transformation of a community, the strengthening of relationships, or the personal growth of the giver, generosity is a force that nurtures and uplifts everyone involved. By giving, individuals contribute to the collective well-being, creating a cycle of kindness and compassion that can ripple through society, inspiring more people to engage in acts of generosity. The impact of generosity is limitless, proving that it has the power to shape a better, more connected world for all.

CHAPTER 3

The Power of Getting

In many cultures around the world, the value of giving is emphasized as a virtuous act, often regarded as the cornerstone of moral behavior and community health. From a young age, individuals are taught that helping others, whether through charity, sharing resources, or offering emotional support, is a reflection of one's strength and character. This belief has deep roots in various religious teachings, societal norms, and cultural practices that celebrate selflessness and sacrifice. In many ways, this emphasis on giving fosters empathy, kindness, and cooperation. However, alongside this cultural emphasis on giving, there is often an implicit message that receiving help, whether it be material, emotional, or even intellectual, is secondary or, in some cases, a sign of weakness or dependency.

At first glance, receiving may seem passive, perhaps even selfish. But in reality, the act of receiving is deeply transformative. It is just as powerful as giving, and without it, the cycle of growth and reciprocity that sustains a healthy community cannot function. Receiving is not a sign of dependence; rather, it is an act of openness, humility, and trust—qualities that are crucial for personal and collective development.

The idea that receiving is inferior to giving is evident in many cultures where self-sufficiency is considered a virtue. For example, in some Western cultures, the "pull-yourself-up-by-the-bootstraps" mentality is common, where individuals are expected to manage their problems independently and are often reluctant to ask for help. This notion is ingrained in society through stories of self-made individuals who succeed through sheer determination, reinforcing the belief that strength comes from standing alone. Similarly, in many Eastern cultures, the importance of giving—especially to family and community—is stressed, while the idea of receiving is often associated with vulnerability or failure. This belief can lead to feelings of guilt or shame when individuals are in need of help, as they may feel they are not living up to the cultural ideals of strength and independence.

However, in the context of the *give–get–grow* framework, both giving and receiving are essential components of thriving in a community. The act of receiving is not a sign of weakness but a vital part of the equation that allows individuals and communities to grow, connect, and support one another in meaningful ways. It is through receiving that we recognize our own needs, create deeper bonds with others, and find the space to restore and replenish ourselves. Receiving is not about passivity; it is an active process that allows us to learn, grow, and evolve.

Similarly, in the professional world, the ability to receive mentorship or guidance from more experienced individuals is a powerful example of how receiving contributes to personal and communal growth. Many people are hesitant to ask for help at work, fearing they will be perceived as incapable or weak. Yet seeking mentorship or feedback is a way to learn, improve, and contribute more effectively in the long run. A young entrepreneur, for instance, might receive advice from an experienced mentor on how to handle financial difficulties or manage a growing team. In this case, receiving wisdom and knowledge not only helps the individual navigate their challenges more effectively but also strengthens their ability to give back to others as they grow. Over time, they may find themselves in a position to offer the same guidance to someone else, completing the circle of giving and receiving that supports the overall growth of the community.

Embracing the act of receiving also fosters greater self-awareness and humility. It allows us to recognize that we are not infallible and that our well-being is intricately tied to the people around us. When we accept help, we open ourselves up to learning from others, whether it is in the form of guidance, encouragement, or even constructive criticism. In turn, this humility can lead to personal growth and a deeper understanding of ourselves and our place within the larger community. For example, a person who has struggled with self-doubt might receive encouragement from a close friend or colleague, which helps them gain the confidence to pursue new opportunities or overcome challenges they would otherwise avoid. The act of receiving that support not only boosts their confidence but also enhances their sense of connection and belonging.

Ultimately, the *give–get–grow* equation highlights that thriving in a community requires both giving and receiving. It is through giving that we contribute to the well-being of others, but it is through receiving that we enable ourselves and others to grow, learn, and build stronger connections. The power of giving and receiving lies in the balance between these two forces, which together create a healthy, thriving ecosystem of mutual support, care, and growth. By embracing both giving and receiving, we recognize that strength is not about independence but about interdependence—our ability to support one another in ways that foster collective well-being and personal growth.

The Courage to Receive

The courage to receive is a crucial yet often overlooked aspect of personal and communal growth. In a world that frequently emphasizes self-sufficiency, independence, and the virtue of giving, receiving can feel like a vulnerability, a sign of weakness, or even an imposition. However, the ability to graciously accept help, support, or kindness from others is not only an act of courage but also an essential component of thriving in both personal and professional spheres. It requires self-awareness, humility, and the willingness to recognize that, sometimes, we need others to move forward, heal, or grow.

One example of *the courage to receive* can be seen in the context of a person going through a difficult period in their life, such as the loss of a loved one. During such times, people often feel that they must remain strong and composed, not wanting to burden others with their pain. This can make them reluctant to accept help or emotional support, even when they desperately need it. However, the act of receiving support—whether it is through comforting words, practical help with daily tasks, or simply having someone to talk to—requires vulnerability and trust. A person who accepts this help, despite their discomfort, allows themselves the space to grieve and heal. By embracing the support of others, they not only receive comfort but also reinforce the bonds of connection with those who care about them. This act of courage acknowledges that they do not have to bear their burdens alone, and by receiving, they invite others to share in their journey toward healing.

In a professional setting, the courage to receive is often seen when individuals accept mentorship or guidance. In many workplaces, people are hesitant to ask for help for fear of being seen as incapable or incompetent. A person new to a leadership role, for example, may feel intimidated about seeking advice from a more experienced colleague, thinking that it will reflect poorly on their abilities. However, by receiving constructive feedback, advice, or mentorship, the individual can grow, refine their leadership skills, and avoid making costly mistakes. The courage to receive guidance not only helps the individual develop but also strengthens the team, as they become more capable and confident in their role. Moreover, a culture that embraces receiving guidance, instead of equating it with weakness, encourages continuous learning and growth within the organization.

Similarly, in personal relationships, accepting help or emotional support can be challenging, especially for individuals who pride themselves on being independent or self-reliant. For instance, someone who is used to taking care of others may struggle when they need to ask for support themselves, fearing they will appear needy or vulnerable. The courage to receive in such situations involves letting go of pride and embracing the reality that everyone has moments when they need help. This could mean allowing a friend to help with chores when they are feeling overwhelmed or leaning on a partner for emotional support during a stressful time. The act of receiving in these situations fosters deeper intimacy and trust, as it allows the other person to feel valued and appreciated for their care. When we open ourselves to receiving help, we create stronger bonds in our relationships, reinforcing the idea that both giving and receiving are necessary for mutual support.

The courage to receive also plays a vital role in the *give–get–grow* framework. In this dynamic, giving is an essential part of building community and fostering connection, but so is receiving. The ability to receive creates a balanced exchange that allows both parties to grow. For instance, in a volunteer organization, a person who offers their time and energy to help others may also benefit from the experience. They may receive new perspectives, a sense of fulfillment, and skills that help them grow personally and professionally. Likewise, the recipients of their generosity benefit from the care and support, creating a cycle of giving and receiving that strengthens the community as a whole. By receiving, individuals not only nourish their own well-being but also contribute to the well-being of the community, creating a continuous loop of growth and support.

In conclusion, *the courage to receive* is not just about overcoming the discomfort of asking for help; it is about recognizing that our growth, well-being, and connection with others are enhanced through receiving. Whether it's emotional support, mentorship, constructive feedback, or physical care, receiving allows us to heal, grow, and thrive. It requires vulnerability, humility, and a willingness to trust in others. When we embrace the courage to receive, we open ourselves up to new possibilities, stronger relationships, and personal growth, ultimately contributing to a more interconnected and supportive community.

The Emotional Power of Receiving

The emotional power of receiving is a profound yet often overlooked aspect of human connection and growth. While giving is widely celebrated for its generosity and selflessness, receiving holds a unique emotional power that can deeply impact both the giver and the receiver. Embracing the act of receiving requires vulnerability, trust, and humility, and when done with openness, it can create a powerful emotional exchange that strengthens relationships, fosters empathy, and promotes healing. The emotional act of receiving is not just about taking; it's about allowing oneself to be seen, supported, and cared for, creating deeper bonds of connection.

One of the most significant emotional impacts of receiving is the sense of validation and worth it can provide. When someone offers help or support—whether it's a listening ear, a thoughtful gift, or a kind gesture—it can make the receiver feel valued and recognized. This is particularly true in moments when individuals are facing challenges or emotional struggles. For example, someone going through a tough time, such as a job loss or a personal setback, might feel isolated or invisible. When a friend reaches out to offer emotional support, whether through a simple message, a phone call, or an invitation to spend time together, the receiver is not just being helped; they are being seen. This act of receiving reminds the individual that they matter, that others care, and that they are not alone in their journey. The emotional power of receiving in such cases is the reaffirmation of their value as a person, which can be immensely healing.

Additionally, the emotional power of receiving extends to the realm of personal growth and healing. In times of emotional or physical pain, the ability to receive help from others can significantly aid in the recovery process. Many individuals struggle with accepting help during times of distress, whether it's because they fear burdening others or because they feel they should be able to manage on their own. Yet, when someone allows themselves to receive care—whether through therapy, medical attention, or even a friend helping with daily tasks—they create space for healing. For instance, a person recovering from surgery or a serious illness may feel overwhelmed by the demands of recovery. By allowing others to assist with meals, errands, or simply providing companionship, they experience a reduction in stress and a sense of emotional relief. This exchange not only aids in physical recovery but also nurtures emotional resilience, as the person learns to lean on others for support and experiences the comfort of communal care.

Moreover, the emotional power of receiving can be seen in how it helps break down barriers and foster empathy. When we allow ourselves to receive, we also allow ourselves to be vulnerable, which can inspire others to do the same. In communities or social settings, the act of receiving can create a ripple effect, encouraging others to open up and accept help when they need it. For instance, in a group of friends, if one person shares a difficult experience and is met with empathy and support from the others, it encourages an environment where vulnerability is safe and acceptable. This exchange of emotional support strengthens the community as a whole, as each individual feels more comfortable both giving and receiving support. The emotional power of receiving, in this sense, extends beyond the individual and creates a collective sense of understanding, compassion, and connection.

The emotional power of receiving can also be experienced on a deeper, more spiritual level. In various religious and spiritual traditions, receiving is not just about material or physical assistance; it is seen as an exchange with the universe, a higher power, or the community. Many individuals find profound emotional fulfillment in receiving blessings or guidance from a spiritual leader or in accepting acts of kindness from strangers. For instance, in some cultures, receiving a small gift or a simple gesture of goodwill can have deep emotional meaning, as it reinforces the belief that we are all interconnected and that life's blessings come in many forms. This emotional exchange through receiving can bring a sense of peace, gratitude, and purpose, as individuals recognize their place within a larger, supportive whole.

Finally, the emotional power of receiving extends to its ability to foster self-compassion. When individuals are able to receive help, they acknowledge that they are deserving of care and kindness. In a society that often pressures people to be self-reliant and stoic, allowing oneself to receive can be an act of self-love. For example, a person who has been emotionally exhausted by overwork may choose to take a day off, accepting care from friends or family members who encourage them to rest. This act of receiving care not only restores their energy but also teaches them the importance of taking care of themselves. Through this, they can better understand the value of self-compassion and the emotional necessity of receiving in maintaining overall well-being.

In conclusion, *the emotional power of receiving* lies in its ability to nurture healing, strengthen relationships, foster empathy, and encourage personal growth. Whether through emotional support, constructive feedback, or the simple act of allowing others to care for us, receiving is a transformative exchange that deepens our connections and enriches our lives. By embracing the vulnerability that comes with receiving, we unlock new layers of emotional strength, resilience, and compassion, both for ourselves and for those around us.

Receiving Creates Space for Others to Give

Receiving creates space for others to give is a powerful and often overlooked aspect of human interaction that contributes to building deeper, more meaningful relationships. While giving is widely celebrated, the act of receiving has a transformative effect on both the giver and the receiver, allowing for a cyclical flow of support and kindness. When we receive, we not only take in help or care, but we also give others the opportunity to express generosity, compassion, and goodwill. This reciprocal exchange creates a space for mutual growth, deepening emotional bonds and strengthening communities.

One of the clearest examples of how receiving creates space for others to give can be seen in personal relationships, particularly in times of need. When someone is going through a difficult experience—whether it's a health issue, a personal loss, or a major life transition—the natural instinct might be to withdraw or refuse help out of pride or a desire to protect others. However, by allowing oneself to receive help, whether it's emotional support, practical assistance, or just a listening ear, the receiver creates an opportunity for others to give. In doing so, they also empower the giver to express care, concern, and empathy.

In professional settings, receiving also creates opportunities for others to give in meaningful ways. For instance, an employee who is struggling with a project may feel reluctant to ask for help, fearing they might appear weak or incompetent. Yet, by accepting support from a colleague or mentor, they are not only solving their own problem but also giving the other person an opportunity to contribute their expertise, time, or wisdom. When an employee receives feedback or assistance, the mentor or colleague feels validated in their role, knowing that their input is appreciated and has made a positive impact. The act of receiving thus creates a collaborative environment where both parties benefit. It fosters a culture of support, learning, and mutual respect that can enhance productivity and morale.

Similarly, in community-driven efforts such as volunteer organizations or charity work, receiving can create a space for others to give, both materially and emotionally. For example, during a natural disaster, those affected by the calamity often receive food, shelter, and medical aid from humanitarian organizations and volunteers. While the recipients are grateful for the help, their acceptance of assistance also allows the volunteers and organizations to fulfill their mission and purpose. Volunteers often find a deep sense of fulfillment in helping others, as it gives them the chance to make a tangible difference in someone's life. The act of receiving not only benefits the recipient but also nourishes the givers by allowing them to express their compassion and care. This exchange strengthens community ties and reinforces the idea that helping others is a shared responsibility.

On a personal level, receiving can also create space for others to give in the form of emotional support. When someone is facing emotional turmoil—be it due to stress, sadness, or anxiety—they might be hesitant to reach out for help, fearing that they will burden others. However, when they allow themselves to receive comfort, whether through talking with a friend, accepting a kind gesture, or simply expressing their emotions, they offer others the opportunity to show love and compassion. A friend who listens to someone's struggles may not only help them process their emotions but may also gain a sense of emotional fulfillment from being there for them. By creating space for others to give emotionally, both parties benefit: The receiver feels heard and understood, and the giver experiences the emotional reward of helping someone they care about.

In another context, receiving can create space for others to give their talents or knowledge. In a collaborative setting—whether it's a creative project, a business venture, or a school assignment—one person's willingness to receive input or ideas allows others to contribute their skills, perspectives, and expertise. For instance, a writer working on a manuscript might hesitate to share their work for fear of criticism or rejection. But by receiving feedback from others—whether from editors, colleagues, or peers—they open up the opportunity for their collaborators to give constructive criticism, new ideas, and support. This exchange often leads to a stronger final product and a deeper sense of teamwork. Similarly, in a classroom setting, when a student accepts help from a teacher or classmate, it not only aids their learning but also allows the teacher or peer to give the gift of knowledge and encouragement.

In family dynamics, receiving creates space for family members to bond through mutual care and support. For example, when parents receive support from their children, whether in the form of small acts of help or emotional understanding, it strengthens the parent–child relationship. It demonstrates to the children that their contributions matter and are appreciated, which reinforces a sense of purpose and belonging within the family. At the same time, parents who allow themselves to receive love, affection, and assistance from their children are teaching them that caring for one another is a shared responsibility that enriches the entire family unit. These exchanges not only deepen familial connections but also foster a culture of mutual care, reinforcing the importance of both giving and receiving within the family structure.

Ultimately, receiving creates space for others to give because it allows for a cycle of generosity, support, and emotional connection. Whether in personal relationships, professional settings, or community efforts, the act of receiving empowers others to step forward, share their resources, and express their care. It fosters an environment of interdependence where both giving and receiving are seen as integral to personal and collective well-being. By allowing ourselves to receive, we not only benefit from the kindness and support of others but also contribute to the well-being of those around us by offering them the opportunity to give.

The Interdependence of Giving and Getting

The interdependence of giving and getting is a foundational concept in building strong relationships, thriving communities, and fostering personal growth. At its core, this idea emphasizes that giving and getting are not separate or opposing actions but are instead deeply interconnected, creating a reciprocal flow that benefits everyone involved. When we give, we create opportunities for others to give in return, and when we get, we provide others with the opportunity to offer help, kindness, or support. This dynamic builds a cycle of mutual exchange that nourishes both individuals and communities, strengthening bonds and creating a sense of shared purpose.

In personal relationships, the interdependence of giving and getting is crucial for emotional well-being. For example, in a friendship, one person may offer a listening ear and support during a challenging time. By giving this emotional care, the giver not only helps their friend through the hardship but also strengthens their bond. However, the act of getting this support is equally important—it provides the person with comfort, reassurance, and a sense of connection. Moreover, the person might feel inspired to give back, offering their own support when the giver faces challenges in the future. This mutual exchange creates a balanced, interdependent relationship, where both individuals give and get in turn, fostering trust, loyalty, and emotional closeness.

In the workplace, the interdependence of giving and getting is vital for creating a collaborative and productive environment. Employees often give their time, skills, and expertise to contribute to the success of a project or organization. For example, one colleague might volunteer to help another complete a complex task, sharing their knowledge and resources. This act of giving not only supports the team but also strengthens professional relationships and encourages a sense of camaraderie. On the flip side, getting help or advice from others is essential for personal and professional growth. For instance, when someone gets mentorship from a more experienced colleague, they gain valuable insights and guidance that enhance their skills and performance. This exchange of giving and getting benefits both parties: The mentor feels fulfilled by sharing their expertise, and the mentee benefits from learning and developing. Ultimately, the interdependence of giving and getting in the workplace leads to a more cohesive, efficient, and supportive team dynamic.

In the context of social justice and humanitarian efforts, the interdependence of giving and getting is equally vital. For example, humanitarian aid workers may give their time and resources to support communities in crisis, such as those affected by natural disasters or conflict. While the workers provide immediate assistance, the communities they serve also give back in subtle but powerful ways. These communities often show immense resilience, wisdom, and gratitude, which can inspire the aid workers and motivate them to continue their efforts. In some cases, individuals from affected communities may eventually become part of the relief efforts, giving back once they have recovered or found support themselves. This cycle of giving and getting not only helps meet immediate needs but also empowers communities to rebuild, grow, and support others in the future.

In family dynamics, the interdependence of giving and getting is crucial for maintaining healthy, supportive relationships. Parents, for example, often give their time, energy, and resources to raise their children, ensuring their emotional, physical, and educational needs are met. However, the act of giving is not one-sided; parents also get emotional rewards from their children, such as love, affection, and the joy of watching them grow. Over time, children also begin to give back, whether through their actions, appreciation, or by offering help when parents are in need. For instance, as children grow older, they may assist with household chores or offer emotional support when their parents face challenges. This mutual exchange strengthens the family unit, fostering a sense of care, respect, and connection.

In summary, *the interdependence of giving and getting* is a dynamic that strengthens individuals, relationships, and communities. By giving, we contribute to the well-being of others, and by getting, we allow others the opportunity to give and share their support. This reciprocal exchange is vital for personal growth, community resilience, and the development of meaningful connections. Whether in our personal lives, workplaces, communities, or global efforts, the act of both giving and getting creates a cycle of mutual aid, deepening our relationships and fostering a sense of shared responsibility and connection.

Embracing the Power of Getting

Embracing the power of getting highlights the importance of recognizing that receiving—whether it's help, support, wisdom, or love—plays a vital role in the cycle of human connection and growth. While giving is often celebrated and seen as the more virtuous act, getting is equally powerful and essential to building a balanced and thriving community. By embracing the power of getting, we not only allow ourselves to benefit from the kindness and generosity of others but also create space for others to experience the joy and fulfillment that comes from offering their help. The act of receiving is not a sign of weakness but a vital part of the reciprocal flow that strengthens relationships, fosters growth, and builds resilience.

One clear example of the power of getting can be seen in times of personal struggle or hardship. When someone is facing a life challenge—whether it's illness, financial difficulties, or emotional distress—it can be difficult to ask for help. Society often emphasizes self-reliance, and there can be a sense of shame or guilt associated with receiving assistance. However, by allowing ourselves to get help from others—whether through emotional support, practical assistance, or financial aid—we not only ease our own burden but also give others the opportunity to express care, compassion, and generosity. A person who is supported during a difficult time may feel a deep sense of relief and gratitude, which in turn strengthens their connection to the giver. For instance, a person going through a tough time might receive help from a friend who cooks meals for them or offers a listening ear. This act of getting help allows the recipient to heal, reflect, and grow stronger. Over time, they may be able to give back to the friend when the need arises, creating a cycle of mutual support.

In the professional world, embracing the power of getting can be transformative for both personal development and organizational success. Employees who receive mentorship, feedback, or guidance from more experienced colleagues are able to grow in their careers and develop new skills. This type of reciprocal relationship benefits both parties: The mentor feels fulfilled by sharing their knowledge, and the mentee gains valuable insights that improve their performance. In one example, a junior employee who is new to a field might feel unsure of their abilities. By getting feedback from a more experienced colleague, they not only enhance their skills but also build their confidence. In return, the mentor benefits from seeing the growth and success of the mentee, and they feel valued for their contributions. This exchange fosters a supportive and collaborative work environment where both giving and getting are seen as integral to success.

The power of getting is also evident in community-based efforts, where individuals receive support from their peers, organizations, and social networks. For instance, during times of crisis—such as natural disasters or economic hardships—communities come together to offer aid to those in need. However, it's important to remember that receiving this help is not a one-way transaction. By allowing oneself to get help, a person not only eases their own struggle but also strengthens the community as a whole. When a person gets assistance, whether in the form of food, shelter, or emotional support, it creates a sense of interconnectedness and solidarity. This sense of shared responsibility allows others to step forward and give, knowing that their actions will have a positive impact. For example, during a flood, people who receive food, clothing, or shelter from relief organizations may eventually have the opportunity to give back once they have recovered. They may donate money to future disaster relief efforts or volunteer their time, continuing the cycle of getting and giving. By embracing the power of getting, individuals contribute to the overall resilience of the community, fostering a collective spirit of care and support.

Furthermore, in intimate relationships, embracing the power of getting strengthens bonds and fosters mutual care. In romantic partnerships, for instance, partners who are open to getting emotional support, affection, or even physical help from each other build a deeper sense of trust and intimacy. A partner who is willing to get help with household responsibilities or emotional labor allows the other to give their time and attention, making the relationship feel more balanced. This dynamic of giving and getting nurtures a sense of partnership where both individuals feel valued and supported. For instance, one partner might get help from the other when dealing with work stress or family issues. In turn, the partner offering support feels appreciated and needed, reinforcing the emotional connection between them. This mutual exchange enhances the overall health of the relationship, proving that both giving and getting are essential.

In sum, *embracing the power of getting* is not about being passive or dependent; rather, it is about recognizing the value in allowing others to contribute to our well-being, growth, and success. By getting help, advice, support, or love, we create space for others to express their generosity and kindness, thus deepening relationships and fostering a sense of interconnection. This cyclical flow of giving and getting enriches our lives, helps us overcome challenges, and builds stronger, more resilient communities. Just as we offer to give to others, we must also be willing to get in return, as this balance allows us to thrive and grow together.

CHAPTER 4

The Cycle of Growth

The *cycle of growth* is not merely a concept but an essential part of the fabric of human experience. It reflects how growth is nurtured through interconnected actions and mutual support, creating a dynamic where every step forward is met with the opportunity for further development. This ongoing cycle teaches us that progress is not achieved through solitary effort alone, but through a series of exchanges—whether it's giving knowledge, receiving guidance, or offering support in times of need. The cycle reinforces the idea that growth is both an individual and collective experience, one that thrives on cooperation, collaboration, and reciprocal generosity.

Take, for example, the journey of personal health. When someone begins a fitness regimen, they *give* their commitment, time, and energy to improve their physical well-being. Along the way, they *get* support from personal trainers, fitness communities, or health professionals who offer expertise, motivation, and feedback. This guidance helps them navigate their challenges and stay on course. As their health improves, they might share their experiences with others, giving tips or encouragement to those who are just starting their journey. In this way, their growth not only benefits them but also positively impacts the people around them, creating a ripple effect of health and well-being.

Similarly, in creative fields like art or writing, the cycle of growth is equally important. A writer, for example, may *give* time to developing their craft, pouring effort into writing and refining their skills. In return, they *get* feedback from readers, editors, and peers, which helps them improve and evolve their work. The cycle doesn't stop there—the writer then shares their refined work with others, inspiring new ideas and creativity in the process. This exchange of giving and receiving fuels artistic growth, not only for the individual but also for the broader community of creators and appreciators.

The cycle of growth is also fundamental to overcoming challenges. When faced with adversity, individuals often find that they must rely on both giving and getting to succeed. For instance, during a period of financial struggle, someone might give their time and energy to help others in need, which helps them keep a sense of purpose and stay grounded. In return, they might get assistance from family, friends, or community organizations, allowing them to recover and rebuild their financial standing. As they recover, they often find themselves in a position to give back to those who helped them, continuing the cycle of support and resilience.

Moreover, the cycle of growth nurtures not only external achievements but also personal development. It encourages a mindset of continuous learning, where every experience—whether of giving or getting—is seen as an opportunity for growth. People who embrace this cycle develop a deeper sense of empathy, gratitude, and understanding. They learn the value of both giving and receiving, recognizing that growth comes not just from individual effort but from the relationships and exchanges that occur along the way. For instance, someone who has received mentorship might eventually become a mentor themselves, passing on the knowledge and guidance they once received. This perpetuates the cycle, ensuring that the wisdom, skills, and support continue to flow, benefiting future generations.

Ultimately, the cycle of growth teaches us that growth is an ongoing, interconnected process that thrives on mutual exchange. Every act of giving, whether small or large, creates opportunities for receiving—and vice versa—allowing individuals, communities, and organizations to evolve. Through this reciprocal cycle, we learn that growth is not just about what we achieve individually but about how we contribute to the growth of others, and how we allow ourselves to be shaped by the support, encouragement, and wisdom of those around us. This interconnected cycle is the heart of true progress, fostering a world where everyone has the potential to thrive, learn, and contribute.

The Interconnectedness of Giving, Getting, and Growing

The interconnectedness of giving, getting, and growing highlights how these three actions are not separate entities but are deeply intertwined, forming a cycle that propels both individuals and communities forward. The act of giving creates the space for others to give in return, while getting allows us to grow by receiving support, insights, and opportunities. In turn, this growth enables us to give more, creating a continuous loop that strengthens relationships, nurtures personal development, and fosters collective well-being.

Consider a mentor–mentee relationship as an example. A mentor gives their time, expertise, and wisdom to guide a less experienced individual. This act of giving allows the mentee to gain valuable knowledge, skills, and insights, enabling them to grow personally and professionally. However, the mentee's growth doesn't just benefit them; it allows them to *give* back to the mentor by offering fresh perspectives, gratitude, or even sharing their own evolving experiences. The cycle continues as the mentee, having grown in their own right, eventually becomes a mentor themselves, passing on the knowledge they received to the next generation. Through this dynamic exchange of giving, getting, and growing, both individuals evolve, benefiting from each other in ways that would not have been possible in isolation.

In a workplace setting, the interconnectedness of giving, getting, and growing is crucial for creating a thriving team environment. A seasoned employee may *give* their time and expertise to help a new colleague navigate a complex project. By getting the support of their more experienced peers, the newcomer can grow in their role, learning essential skills and strategies. This growth, in turn, enables the new employee to *give* back to the team, perhaps by sharing new ideas, fresh approaches, or offering assistance in future projects. As the cycle continues, each individual contributes to the overall success of the team, while also benefiting from the knowledge and support of others, creating a collaborative atmosphere that fosters mutual growth.

Another example of the interconnectedness of giving, getting, and growing can be found in the educational sphere. Teachers give their knowledge, patience, and dedication to students, helping them develop academically and emotionally. In return, students get the tools they need to succeed and grow into knowledgeable and capable individuals. However, the cycle doesn't end there. As students grow, they often *give* back to their teachers through feedback, participation, and showing appreciation for the learning process. Furthermore, as some students progress in their careers, they may return to teach the next generation, completing the cycle of giving, getting, and growing. The exchange of knowledge and experiences between teachers and students is not just a one-time event but an ongoing, dynamic process that benefits both parties.

At a personal level, the interconnectedness of giving, getting, and growing is a key element of emotional and psychological well-being. A person who is struggling with a difficult time may get support from friends, family, or counselors. This act of getting support doesn't just help the individual overcome their challenge; it also creates the potential for emotional growth. As they heal and develop greater resilience, they are better equipped to give back—offering support to others who are going through similar struggles. For example, someone who has gone through grief and received comfort from others may, in turn, become a source of comfort for someone else who has lost a loved one. The act of getting support allows for personal growth, which then enables individuals to give back, continuing the cycle of support, empathy, and connection.

In summary, *the interconnectedness of giving, getting, and growing* is a foundational principle that strengthens individuals and communities. Each action is a catalyst for the other—giving opens the door for getting, which in turn leads to growth. Whether it's in mentorship, workplace collaboration, community service, education, or personal relationships, the continuous cycle of giving, getting, and growing fosters an environment where everyone has the opportunity to thrive, contribute, and evolve. This dynamic process demonstrates that growth is not a solitary achievement but a collective effort, where each person's contributions enrich the lives of others and, in turn, enable their own development.

How Growth Transforms Individuals

Growth, in its many forms—whether personal, professional, or emotional—has the power to transform individuals in profound ways. It's a continuous process that shapes our mindset, enhances our abilities, and enriches our lives. When individuals embrace growth, they are not merely evolving in their skills or knowledge but are also developing resilience, emotional intelligence, and a deeper understanding of themselves and the world around them. The transformation that occurs through growth isn't always immediately visible, but over time, it leads to profound shifts in behavior, perspective, and capacity.

One powerful example of how growth transforms individuals can be seen in the process of learning a new skill or mastering a craft. Take, for example, someone who decides to learn how to play the piano. At the start, the process is difficult. They struggle with hand coordination, reading music, and keeping rhythm. But as they continue practicing, they experience incremental improvements. The act of learning, despite initial setbacks, builds not only their musical abilities but also their perseverance and patience. Over time, their confidence grows, and they begin to express themselves more freely through music, experiencing a sense of accomplishment and personal pride. This transformation extends beyond the musical domain—it changes how they approach challenges in other areas of their life. The growth they experienced as a musician encourages them to tackle obstacles with greater resilience and a growth-oriented mindset, believing that continued effort can lead to success.

Emotional and personal growth is another powerful way in which individuals are transformed. One example can be seen in individuals overcoming significant life challenges, such as the loss of a loved one, battling addiction, or recovering from trauma. These experiences, while painful, often serve as catalysts for deep personal growth. A person who has experienced profound loss may initially feel overwhelmed by grief and sorrow. However, through support, therapy, self-reflection, and time, they begin to grow emotionally. They may develop greater empathy, a more profound sense of gratitude for life, and a deeper connection to others. The transformation often involves learning how to cope with pain, discovering new strengths, and finding meaning in life despite adversity. This growth enables them to approach future challenges with a sense of resilience and hope, transforming their outlook on life.

Growth can also have a profound impact on an individual's relationships. Someone who has spent years avoiding difficult conversations might, through personal growth, learn how to communicate more openly and effectively. By improving their self-awareness and emotional intelligence, they begin to understand the needs and emotions of others better. As a result, their relationships with family, friends, and colleagues deepen, leading to more fulfilling and meaningful connections. For example, a person who once struggled with expressing vulnerability might, through growth, become more open with their emotions. This shift not only strengthens their personal relationships but also allows them to build trust and create deeper bonds with others. Their growth as an individual transforms how they interact with the world and enriches the quality of their relationships.

Another example of how growth transforms individuals can be seen in the way people approach leadership. Someone who begins their career with little interest in leadership may, over time, develop an understanding of what it means to guide and inspire others. Through education, mentorship, and hands-on experience, they learn the value of empathy, listening, and collaboration. As they grow, they adopt a leadership style that encourages growth in others, empowering their teams and creating environments where people can thrive. The individual's transformation from a contributor to a leader is a direct result of their willingness to learn, adapt, and grow, and it changes the way they approach challenges, decision making, and interpersonal dynamics.

In sum, growth has the power to transform individuals in ways that extend far beyond skill development or personal achievements. It reshapes how people view themselves and the world around them. Growth builds resilience, emotional intelligence, and a deep sense of connection to others. It helps individuals evolve from one stage of life to the next with greater self-awareness, confidence, and capacity. Whether through learning new skills, overcoming adversity, improving relationships, or stepping into leadership roles, growth continuously pushes individuals toward becoming better versions of themselves. This transformation is not always easy, but it is always worthwhile, as it enables people to lead richer, more fulfilling lives while contributing to the growth and well-being of others.

Growth as a Collective Process

Growth is often seen as a deeply personal journey, but its true power lies in its collective nature. While individual growth is essential, it's the interdependence between people that fosters a deeper and more impactful transformation. Whether within communities, organizations, or societies at large, growth is a collective process—each individual's development contributes to the larger evolution of the whole. As people come together to share their strengths, knowledge, and experiences, they collectively grow, leading to outcomes that none could achieve alone.

One powerful example of growth as a collective process can be found in the development of a community. When individuals within a community come together to address a common issue—such as poverty, education, or environmental sustainability—they not only contribute their time and resources but also learn from one another. For instance, a group of people may decide to tackle homelessness in their city. Each person brings a unique skill set to the table: Some may have experience in social work, others in fundraising, and some in advocacy. Through collaboration, these individuals grow in their understanding of how complex issues can be solved when multiple perspectives and approaches are combined. As they work together, they not only build tangible solutions but also strengthen relationships within the community, foster empathy, and deepen their shared commitment to the cause. The collective effort results in a positive transformation for everyone involved, and the ripple effect of that growth can spread, improving the broader community over time.

In the workplace, growth as a collective process is evident in high-performing teams. Rather than relying on the isolated contributions of individual employees, a successful team thrives because each person's strengths are integrated and leveraged. For example, in a project team within a tech company, one person may be excellent at coding, another at problem-solving, and another at project management. As they work together, they not only contribute to the project's success but also learn from one another, expanding their skills and perspectives in the process. The team's collective growth happens when individuals move beyond their personal development and learn how to collaborate effectively, pooling their knowledge and experiences to achieve common goals. This collaboration leads to innovation, efficiency, and success—outcomes that would not have been possible if the team members worked in isolation.

In educational settings, growth as a collective process plays out when students and educators engage in a shared learning experience. A classroom is more than just a place for individual achievement; it's a space where growth happens collectively. Students learn not only from their teachers but also from one another. A group discussion, for example, can help students see a concept from different viewpoints and deepen their understanding in ways they might not have achieved alone. Group projects and collaborative assignments encourage students to share ideas, challenge each other's thinking, and develop problem-solving skills together. In these environments, the growth of the individual is intertwined with the growth of the group, and the knowledge gained through collective interaction becomes more comprehensive and enriched. The teacher, too, grows from the feedback and insights provided by students, shaping the direction of future lessons and fostering an adaptive learning environment.

In the context of global challenges, such as climate change or public health crises, collective growth is essential. Addressing such complex issues requires cooperation across nations, organizations, and communities. Take, for example, the global response to the COVID-19 pandemic. Different countries, health organizations, and scientists worked together, sharing data, research, and resources to develop vaccines and strategies for managing the crisis. The collective process of learning from one another, combining expertise, and working in unison led to the rapid development of lifesaving treatments and policies. On a smaller scale, local communities worked together to support vulnerable individuals, providing food, medical assistance, and emotional support. The pandemic highlighted how collective growth—through collaboration, knowledge-sharing, and mutual support—can lead to solutions that are greater than the sum of their parts.

The idea of growth as a collective process also extends to the broader social fabric, where societal norms and values evolve. For instance, as society grows in its understanding of diversity, inclusion, and equity, individuals who once held limited or prejudiced views are challenged to expand their perspectives. Through collective dialogue, education, and activism, societal growth occurs, leading to greater acceptance and justice. This shift in values impacts individuals on a personal level, encouraging them to reexamine their beliefs and adopt more inclusive practices. The collective transformation in attitudes and behaviors, whether on a small or large scale, leads to a more just and harmonious society.

In conclusion, growth as a collective process underscores the idea that individual development is deeply intertwined with the growth of the groups, organizations, and communities we belong to. Whether in the workplace, in educational settings, in social movements, or in our personal lives, growth is nurtured by shared experiences, collaboration, and mutual support. It's not just about what one person can achieve, but about how collective efforts build upon one another to create deeper and more sustainable change. Through collaboration and interdependence, growth becomes a powerful force that can transform not just individuals, but entire communities and societies.

The Role of Feedback in Growth

Feedback is a crucial component of the growth process, acting as a mirror that reflects our actions, behaviors, and results, offering insights into areas where we excel and those that require improvement. It serves as a tool for self-awareness, guiding individuals toward making informed adjustments and continuously progressing. Whether in personal development, professional environments, or educational settings, feedback provides essential information that shapes growth, helping individuals refine their skills, strengthen their relationships, and overcome challenges.

In the workplace, feedback is often the difference between stagnation and improvement. When employees receive constructive feedback, they gain a clear understanding of their strengths and areas for development. For example, a team member who receives feedback on their presentation skills might learn that their delivery is strong, but they need to improve on maintaining eye contact with the audience to appear more engaged. This specific feedback helps the individual focus their efforts on improving a particular aspect of their communication, which can ultimately enhance their overall performance and confidence. Over time, regular feedback allows individuals to continuously refine their abilities, adapt to new expectations, and grow professionally.

Similarly, feedback is a powerful driver of growth in educational settings. Teachers who provide thoughtful and constructive feedback to students don't just highlight mistakes—they offer insights into how those mistakes can be corrected and what steps the student can take to improve. For instance, a student writing an essay might receive feedback on their thesis statement, with suggestions on how to make their argument more clear and compelling. This kind of feedback encourages the student to think critically about their work and make adjustments, fostering a deeper understanding of the subject matter. When feedback is delivered in a positive, constructive way, it motivates students to take ownership of their learning and apply themselves more diligently, thus enhancing their growth and development.

The feedback loop is also crucial for personal growth in the form of self-reflection. While external feedback from others is invaluable, individuals can also learn and grow by giving themselves honest feedback. This self-assessment can happen after a project, a difficult conversation, or a challenging experience. By reflecting on what went well and what could have been done differently, individuals gain insight into their own behaviors, mindset, and actions. For example, after a challenging meeting at work, a person might reflect on their approach to communication and realize that they were too passive in expressing their opinions. This self-feedback encourages them to develop better strategies for asserting themselves in future meetings. Over time, self-reflection helps individuals to take ownership of their growth, fostering greater self-awareness and personal development.

In the realm of creative endeavors, feedback plays a pivotal role in helping artists, writers, and performers improve their craft. For instance, a writer may share their manuscript with peers or editors for feedback. The feedback they receive can help them identify weak plot points, inconsistencies in character development, or areas where the pacing falters. This feedback not only enhances the final product but also sharpens the writer's skills, helping them understand how their audience perceives their work. The feedback loop in creative processes often leads to incremental improvements that, over time, can elevate an artist's craft to new heights. Similarly, musicians or visual artists benefit from constructive criticism in perfecting their technique or expanding their creative range. Feedback offers valuable external perspectives that can inspire new ideas, refine skills, and fuel personal growth in these fields.

In all these scenarios, the key to effective feedback lies not only in the content but also in the manner in which it is delivered. Feedback should be specific, actionable, and supportive rather than vague, punitive, or overly critical. When feedback is delivered with empathy and an intention to help the recipient improve, it fosters a safe environment where individuals feel encouraged to take risks, make mistakes, and learn. In turn, they are more likely to internalize the feedback and apply it to their growth journey.

In conclusion, feedback is an indispensable tool for growth. Whether it's received in a professional context, in personal relationships, or through self-reflection, feedback provides the essential information individuals need to evolve, refine their skills, and overcome obstacles. By fostering a culture of constructive feedback, individuals and communities can build a foundation for continuous learning, innovation, and development. Ultimately, feedback acts as a catalyst for growth, guiding individuals toward greater self-awareness, improved performance, and deeper connections with others.

The Perpetual Motion of the *Give–Get–Grow* Cycle

The *give–get–grow* cycle is a dynamic, perpetual process that shapes not only individuals but entire communities and societies. This cycle is a continual exchange of resources, whether they are material, emotional, intellectual, or relational, and it is through this constant flow of giving, receiving, and growing that both individuals and the communities they belong to thrive. The beauty of this cycle lies in its self-sustaining nature: Each step feeds into the next, creating momentum that propels continuous development and improvement. As individuals give, they receive in return, and through this exchange, they grow. Their growth, in turn, enables them to give more, and so the cycle continues.

At its core, the *give–get–grow* cycle is about balance. It suggests that growth is not a one-sided process but one that requires the interplay of both giving and receiving. For example, when someone mentors another person, they are giving their time, knowledge, and experience. In return, the mentee gains wisdom, skills, and confidence. But, often, the mentor too receives something valuable in this exchange—perhaps a fresh perspective, renewed motivation, or even the satisfaction of knowing they've made a difference. This process of mutual exchange leads to growth for both parties. The mentor's understanding of the subject may deepen through the act of teaching, and the mentee's confidence and abilities grow as they apply what they've learned. This cycle of giving, getting, and growing is repeated with each new interaction, each new opportunity to contribute and learn.

Similarly, in community development, the *give–get–grow* cycle plays a central role in fostering collective progress. When people come together to solve community issues, each individual's contributions help the group move toward a shared goal. A classic example of this is seen in volunteer work. Volunteers often give their time and energy to help a cause, whether it's by cleaning up a local park, tutoring children, or distributing food to the homeless. While these actions help the community, the volunteers themselves receive intangible rewards, such as a sense of accomplishment, fulfillment, and a deeper connection to their community. The community itself grows stronger through the collective efforts of the individuals, who, in turn, are personally transformed by their involvement. This process of giving and receiving creates a sustainable cycle of growth that benefits both the individual and the larger group.

In personal relationships, the *give–get–grow* cycle works similarly. Giving love, support, and care strengthens relationships and fosters mutual growth. For example, when a friend provides emotional support to another during a challenging time, they are offering empathy, time, and understanding. The person receiving this support gains comfort, reassurance, and the emotional tools to cope with their situation. But the giver also experiences growth—they may develop greater emotional intelligence, a sense of connection, and a deeper understanding of their own capacity for compassion. As the relationship deepens, both individuals continue to grow, not only as individuals but as partners in a shared experience, benefiting from the continuous cycle of giving and receiving.

In the end, the perpetual motion of the *give–get–grow* cycle is a powerful reminder of how interconnected we all are. Growth doesn't happen in isolation—it is a product of interaction, exchange, and collaboration. Every act of giving creates space for receiving, and every instance of receiving allows individuals and communities to grow. Through this continuous cycle, individuals, teams, organizations, and even entire societies can thrive, reaching new levels of success, fulfillment, and positive change. The key is recognizing that giving and getting are not opposing forces, but complementary components of a larger, ongoing process of development and transformation. As long as this cycle continues, so too will the growth of those involved.

Growth as the Ultimate Goal

Growth is the ultimate goal because it represents both the journey and the destination of human potential. Whether it occurs at an individual, organizational, or societal level, growth is the driving force that propels us forward, fosters resilience, and leads to deeper fulfillment and understanding. It is the outcome of a well-lived life, rooted in the continuous exchange of giving, getting, and learning. Growth allows us to evolve, adapt, and overcome the challenges that life inevitably presents, and it is through this perpetual process of growth that we can create meaningful and lasting change in ourselves and the world around us.

On a personal level, growth manifests as self-improvement, learning new skills, and expanding our emotional intelligence. For example, someone who learns to manage their time effectively and develops better communication skills is not only enhancing their professional life but also becoming a more balanced and self-aware individual. This personal growth empowers them to take on new challenges, build stronger relationships, and contribute more effectively to their community. Over time, this growth allows individuals to live with greater purpose, contributing to their own well-being as well as the well-being of those around them.

In a professional context, growth is often tied to innovation, skill development, and the ability to adapt to changing circumstances. Companies that prioritize growth foster environments where employees are encouraged to learn, take risks, and share ideas. For instance, an organization that invests in the continuous development of its workforce—through training, mentorship, and constructive feedback—empowers individuals to reach their full potential. As these employees grow, the organization itself grows, becoming more effective, adaptable, and successful. The *give–get–grow* cycle, where employees give their time and effort, receive support and feedback, and grow in their roles, creates a thriving organizational culture that benefits both the individuals and the company as a whole.

Growth also involves the ability to adapt and respond to changing circumstances. In a world that is constantly evolving—whether through technological advancements, shifts in global markets, or societal changes—growth is the key to staying relevant and resilient. Organizations, for example, that embrace innovation and adaptability are more likely to thrive during periods of disruption. When they encourage their teams to experiment, take calculated risks, and learn from failures, they create a culture of continuous improvement. This mindset of growth enables them to stay competitive and respond to challenges with creativity and confidence.

The ultimate goal of growth extends beyond just personal or professional development; it also encompasses the greater good. Growth has the power to create meaningful, positive change on a global scale. Consider the progress made in areas such as public health, environmental conservation, and human rights. In each of these fields, individuals, organizations, and entire communities have worked tirelessly to address pressing issues, resulting in significant strides forward. For example, the global shift toward renewable energy is an outcome of continuous growth in technology, policy, and public awareness. It is not just the growth of the industry that matters, but the growth in collective consciousness about the importance of sustainability. As societies continue to grow in their understanding of environmental issues, they can create lasting change that benefits future generations.

In conclusion, growth is not just an outcome—it is a lifelong pursuit that enriches our lives and the lives of those around us. It is through giving, receiving, and growing that we achieve our fullest potential, and by fostering growth in all aspects of our lives, we contribute to a better, more connected world. Whether it's the growth of an individual, an organization, or a community, the pursuit of growth is what drives us toward progress, understanding, and a more fulfilling existence. As we continue to grow, we empower others to do the same, creating a cycle of growth that transcends generations and leads to a brighter, more prosperous future for all.

CHAPTER 5

Building Trust and Reciprocity

Trust and reciprocity are the cornerstones of meaningful relationships and effective collaboration. These two concepts are deeply interwoven, guiding how we interact with others and how societies function. Trust is the belief that others will act in our best interest, even in the absence of direct oversight, while reciprocity is the expectation that kindness or favors will be returned in some form. Together, they create a cycle of mutual benefit, where individuals feel secure enough to give, share, and collaborate, knowing that their actions will likely be reciprocated in the future.

In personal relationships, trust and reciprocity help build emotional bonds that support long-lasting connections. When trust is present, people are more willing to take risks and be vulnerable with one another, knowing that their actions will be met with understanding and support. This creates a positive feedback loop where acts of kindness and generosity are returned, strengthening the relationship over time. Whether it's friends helping each other or families offering unconditional support, the interplay of trust and reciprocity fosters deep, meaningful connections.

In the professional world, these principles take on even greater significance. In workplaces, teams, and business partnerships, trust enables open communication, encourages collaboration, and enhances productivity. When trust is present, individuals are more likely to share ideas, take on challenges, and invest in the success of the group. Reciprocity in this context fosters cooperation, where employees support one another's growth and success, knowing that their contributions will be recognized and rewarded. This creates an environment where innovation and achievement are possible because individuals are motivated by the understanding that helping others will ultimately benefit them as well.

On a societal level, trust and reciprocity are foundational to the functioning of communities, economies, and governments. When trust is high within a society, people are more likely to engage in cooperative behaviors, share resources, and work toward collective goals. Similarly, reciprocity ensures that individuals contribute to the greater good, knowing that their efforts will be acknowledged and reciprocated. These values enable societies to function smoothly, creating systems of fairness, justice, and mutual respect. As we continue to face global challenges, cultivating trust and reciprocity remains essential for building resilient and thriving communities.

What Is Trust?

Trust is the firm belief or confidence that one person or entity will act in a reliable, fair, and supportive manner. It is an essential foundation for building strong relationships, whether personal, professional, or societal. At its core, trust involves the expectation that others will behave in a way that aligns with shared values, norms, or agreements. It enables people to rely on each other without needing constant reassurance or proof of commitment. Trust is built over time through repeated positive experiences and consistency in behavior. However, trust can also be fragile; once broken, it can be challenging to restore, requiring time, effort, and a genuine commitment to rebuilding confidence.

In personal relationships, trust is crucial for emotional security and intimacy. For example, in a marriage or close friendship, each person trusts that the other will act in ways that are supportive, honest, and dependable. This trust allows individuals to communicate openly, share vulnerabilities, and depend on each other during challenging moments. Without trust, relationships can become strained, as individuals may start to question each other's motives or reliability. If, for instance, one partner breaks the trust by being dishonest or unfaithful, it can lead to emotional harm and may require a significant amount of time and effort to rebuild the relationship.

In the workplace, trust is equally important for collaboration and productivity. Employees trust that their colleagues and managers will be fair, reliable, and supportive. For example, a manager trusts their team to complete tasks on time and deliver quality work, while team members trust that their manager will offer guidance, resources, and recognition. When trust is present, work environments tend to be more harmonious, and individuals are more willing to take on challenges or contribute ideas. However, when trust is violated, such as when a colleague fails to fulfill their responsibilities or a manager acts unfairly, it can lead to a breakdown in communication, decreased morale, and a loss of overall productivity.

On a larger scale, trust is vital for the smooth functioning of societies. Social trust refers to the belief that others will generally behave in ways that contribute to the common good. For example, people trust that drivers will obey traffic laws, which helps prevent accidents and keeps everyone safe. Similarly, individuals trust that public institutions, like the government or police, will act transparently and justly. When social trust is eroded—perhaps due to corruption or unethical behavior—people become less willing to cooperate or follow laws, which can lead to social unrest or disengagement. Therefore, maintaining trust within communities is essential for social harmony and progress.

Trust is also foundational in financial transactions. When a person deposits money in a bank, they trust that the institution will keep their funds safe and return them when needed. Similarly, when businesses and consumers enter into agreements, there is an implicit trust that both parties will honor the terms. For instance, when purchasing goods online, a customer trusts that the seller will deliver the product as promised. If this trust is broken, such as through fraud or nondelivery, it can cause significant damage to the reputation of the involved parties and result in financial loss. In all these contexts, trust plays a pivotal role in facilitating cooperation, reducing uncertainty, and fostering stability. Whether in personal relationships, workplaces, or society at large, trust is a key ingredient in the functioning of healthy and productive systems.

Trust and Vulnerability

Trust and vulnerability are intrinsically connected, as trust often involves allowing oneself to be vulnerable in the presence of others. Vulnerability refers to the willingness to expose one's true self, including weaknesses, fears, and uncertainties, and to rely on others with the expectation that they will not exploit or harm us. Trust creates the space for vulnerability, while vulnerability, in turn, strengthens trust. When we trust someone, we allow ourselves to be vulnerable, and when others handle our vulnerability with care, it deepens our trust in them.

In personal relationships, vulnerability plays a central role in deepening connections. For instance, in a close friendship or romantic relationship, people often share intimate details about their lives, their struggles, and their insecurities. This requires a great deal of trust, as opening up exposes one to potential judgment, rejection, or betrayal. For example, someone may trust their partner enough to confide about their past traumas or fears about the future, knowing that their partner will offer empathy and support rather than criticism. If the partner responds with understanding and reassurance, the trust between them grows, creating a stronger bond. However, if that vulnerability is met with indifference or judgment, it can damage the trust and harm the relationship.

Vulnerability is also crucial in the realm of leadership. Effective leaders often demonstrate vulnerability by being open about their own challenges and shortcomings. This not only humanizes them but also shows that they trust their team to understand and support them. For example, a CEO might openly discuss the difficulties of navigating a challenging market or the pressures of making tough decisions. By showing this kind of vulnerability, they invite their team to share their own challenges and solutions, creating a culture of openness and mutual support. On the other hand, a leader who refuses to show vulnerability—one who maintains a facade of infallibility—might create a culture of fear, where employees are reluctant to speak up or ask for help, ultimately weakening trust within the organization.

In societal and community settings, trust and vulnerability can be seen in the way individuals and groups interact with one another. For instance, in times of crisis, such as a natural disaster or a public health emergency, people often trust their community members to help each other. Vulnerability is present when individuals are willing to rely on others for assistance, knowing that their well-being is at stake. The trust that communities have in each other's willingness to help fosters cooperation and solidarity. However, if there is a breakdown in trust—such as when individuals or institutions take advantage of the vulnerable—it can lead to fear, division, and reluctance to cooperate, undermining the sense of community and shared responsibility.

Trust and vulnerability are essential for creating strong, meaningful relationships in all areas of life. By allowing ourselves to be vulnerable, we take a leap of faith, hoping that others will respond with care, understanding, and support. When that trust is honored, it not only strengthens the bond but encourages further openness and connection. However, when vulnerability is met with betrayal or exploitation, trust can be shattered, and the relationship may be irreparably damaged. Understanding the delicate balance between trust and vulnerability can help individuals build deeper, more resilient connections in their personal, professional, and social lives.

The Cycle of Trust and Reciprocity

This is a dynamic process where trust between individuals or groups leads to reciprocal actions, and these actions, in turn, reinforce and build trust. Initially, trust forms the basis of the relationship, where one party believes the other will act in a way that is beneficial or at least not harmful. This trust prompts reciprocal behavior, where one party offers something positive or supportive, such as assistance, cooperation, or kindness. When the other party reciprocates by responding in a positive way, trust is reinforced, creating a virtuous cycle. Over time, this process of mutual reinforcement leads to greater cooperation and stronger relationships.

In business relationships, for example, trust is essential when a company relies on a supplier to deliver quality products on time. The company's reciprocal action might involve placing a large order or offering favorable payment terms, which builds trust in the supplier's reliability. When the supplier fulfills the order successfully, trust is further strengthened, leading to even more orders and a deeper, more collaborative partnership. Similarly, in friendships, the cycle of trust and reciprocity can be observed when one friend trusts the other to keep a secret or provide support, and in return, the other friend offers emotional support or assistance. As each act of reciprocity is returned with mutual respect, the relationship deepens, strengthening the bond.

In the workplace, the cycle is seen in how colleagues work together. One team member might trust others to meet deadlines and contribute effectively to a project. In return, they help others with tasks or offer their support, which reinforces the initial trust and increases future cooperation. Over time, this process leads to more productive and harmonious teamwork, with individuals becoming more willing to collaborate and share resources. Similarly, in family relationships, trust and reciprocity are key in maintaining strong bonds. A parent trusts a child to follow house rules, and in return, the child respects the rules and may even help with chores. As this cycle continues, both parties grow in mutual respect and cooperation.

Ultimately, the cycle of trust and reciprocity is foundational to the success and longevity of relationships. Whether in personal friendships, workplace dynamics, or international diplomacy, the continuous exchange of trust and reciprocal actions fosters cooperation and strengthens bonds. Understanding and nurturing this cycle can lead to more productive, positive, and enduring relationships in all aspects of life.

The Dangers of Mistrust

Mistrust can have significant and far-reaching consequences in both personal relationships and professional environments. When trust is broken or never established, it can lead to misunderstanding, conflict, inefficiency, and even the complete breakdown of relationships. The dangers of mistrust arise because it disrupts communication, weakens cooperation, and fosters an environment of suspicion and fear. Without trust, individuals or groups are less likely to collaborate effectively, share information openly, or make decisions with confidence. This often leads to increased tension, decreased productivity, and negative emotions such as anxiety, resentment, and frustration.

One of the most immediate dangers of mistrust is its impact on communication. When people do not trust one another, they are less likely to share information openly or be transparent about their intentions. In a workplace, for instance, a lack of trust between colleagues or between employees and management can lead to poor communication. Employees may withhold important information or fail to ask for help when needed, out of fear that sharing will be used against them. Similarly, managers might make decisions without consulting their team, assuming that their employees will not have the best interests of the company at heart. This lack of open communication leads to confusion, missed opportunities, and inefficiency, all of which hinder productivity and team performance. In the long run, the inability to communicate openly and honestly can erode the very foundation of a functioning team or organization.

The dangers of mistrust are particularly evident in business relationships. For instance, if a company and its suppliers do not trust each other, it can lead to disruptions in operations. A supplier may not deliver products on time, fearing that they will not be paid or that the company will cancel the order at the last minute. Similarly, a company may become hesitant to place large orders, fearing that the supplier will not meet quality standards. The resulting lack of cooperation can cause delays, financial losses, and strained business relations. Furthermore, in contract negotiations, if both parties are suspicious of each other's intentions, it can lead to prolonged negotiations, where each side tries to protect their interests at the expense of the other. This prolonged lack of trust can cause missed opportunities for both parties and create an atmosphere of tension and hostility.

In international relations, mistrust between countries can escalate into conflict or even war. For example, during the Cold War, the mistrust between the United States and the Soviet Union led to a global arms race and a series of proxy wars. Each side was suspicious of the other's intentions and sought to outdo the other in military power, leading to instability and a constant threat of nuclear war. Mistrust can also prevent countries from cooperating on global issues such as climate change, trade, or pandemics. When countries do not trust each other, they are less likely to collaborate on shared challenges, leading to fragmented approaches that can exacerbate global problems. The lack of diplomatic trust also fuels tensions in border disputes or territorial conflicts, making it more difficult to negotiate peaceful solutions.

Another significant danger of mistrust is its potential to breed conflict. When people are mistrustful, they tend to interpret actions through a negative lens, leading to misunderstandings and assumptions. For example, if one colleague does not trust another to handle an important project, they may micromanage or second-guess the other's decisions. This can create frustration and resentment, as the mistrusted person feels their competence is being questioned. In families, mistrust can also lead to constant conflict. For instance, if one family member feels that another is not being honest about their finances, this can spark arguments and lead to deeper divisions within the family. In both personal and professional settings, mistrust can lead to a cycle of defensiveness, where individuals or groups become more focused on protecting themselves rather than working together toward a shared goal.

Finally, mistrust can also have significant emotional consequences. It can lead to feelings of insecurity, anxiety, and fear. In the workplace, employees who feel that their managers or colleagues do not trust them may experience stress and dissatisfaction, which can negatively affect their mental health and overall job performance. Similarly, in personal relationships, the constant fear of betrayal or abandonment can lead to emotional exhaustion and a lack of fulfillment. This constant state of vigilance can prevent people from enjoying the positive aspects of their relationships or work, leading to a diminished quality of life.

In conclusion, mistrust is a powerful force that can create a host of problems in relationships, teams, and organizations. It disrupts communication, hinders collaboration, breeds conflict, and causes emotional distress. Whether in the workplace, personal life, or international relations, mistrust can lead to inefficiency, missed opportunities, and long-term damage to relationships. Building and maintaining trust is essential for creating healthy, productive, and harmonious environments. Without trust, the foundation of cooperation is undermined, and the dangers of mistrust can become overwhelming.

The Role of Reciprocity in Building Trust

Reciprocity plays a pivotal role in building trust by creating a sense of mutual benefit and reinforcing positive behaviors between individuals or groups. At its core, reciprocity involves responding to another's actions with similar or favorable actions, which creates a cycle of trust. When one party takes an action that benefits another, the recipient is more likely to return the favor, which not only reinforces the initial action but also strengthens the trust in the relationship. This reciprocal exchange helps build confidence, deepens connections, and encourages future cooperation.

In personal relationships, reciprocity is fundamental to establishing trust. For example, in friendships, one friend might offer support during a difficult time, such as helping with a personal issue or providing emotional support. The recipient, feeling grateful and valued, is likely to reciprocate, whether by offering assistance in the future or being there when the other person faces a challenge. This back-and-forth exchange fosters a deeper bond and strengthens trust. The act of reciprocating shows the individual that their trust in the other is valued, leading to a cycle where both friends feel secure in the relationship and are more likely to continue helping each other. Over time, the consistency of reciprocal actions strengthens the trust that exists between them.

Reciprocity is also essential in team dynamics and workplace cooperation. In a professional setting, one employee might help a colleague meet a tight deadline or share valuable information to solve a problem. In return, the colleague may reciprocate by offering assistance in the future, whether by sharing insights, collaborating on a project, or providing support when needed. This exchange of help and support creates a work environment where team members trust each other's commitment and competence, which ultimately leads to more effective collaboration. When employees feel that their contributions are reciprocated, they are more likely to trust their colleagues and be willing to go the extra mile to ensure the success of the team. Conversely, if one party repeatedly fails to reciprocate, the trust in the team can break down, leading to frustration, decreased cooperation, and a less productive work environment.

However, while reciprocity is crucial in building trust, it's important that it be genuine and consistent. Inauthentic or one-sided reciprocal actions can undermine trust rather than strengthen it. If one party feels that the reciprocity is merely transactional or done out of obligation rather than goodwill, it can breed resentment and suspicion. For instance, if a person feels that their kindness is being used for manipulation or if a company offers perks with the expectation of immediate returns without building a genuine relationship, the cycle of reciprocity may break down. Therefore, reciprocity must be sincere and motivated by a genuine desire to benefit the other person or group, rather than simply seeking to gain something in return.

In conclusion, reciprocity is a cornerstone of trust-building, whether in personal relationships, business dealings, team dynamics, or international relations. By engaging in reciprocal actions, individuals and groups signal that they are reliable, dependable, and invested in the relationship. The act of giving and receiving benefits creates a cycle of trust that deepens connections and fosters a cooperative environment. When reciprocity is genuine and consistent, it leads to stronger, more resilient relationships and encourages future collaboration, making it an essential element in the development of trust.

Cultivating Trust and Reciprocity for Lasting Growth

Cultivating trust and reciprocity is essential for fostering lasting growth, whether in personal relationships, business environments, or broader societal contexts. Trust is the foundation upon which all meaningful connections are built, and reciprocity acts as the dynamic force that sustains and strengthens these bonds over time. When trust is nurtured and reciprocated, it leads to greater cooperation, mutual benefit, and long-term success. Cultivating trust and reciprocity requires conscious effort, consistency, and a genuine commitment to the well-being of others. Through these principles, individuals and organizations can create environments where relationships thrive, opportunities are maximized, and growth is both sustained and fulfilling.

In personal relationships, cultivating trust and reciprocity leads to deeper emotional connections and a more resilient bond. For example, in a marriage, trust forms the foundation of emotional intimacy. When partners trust one another, they feel secure in expressing their vulnerabilities, knowing that their thoughts and feelings will be respected. When one partner offers support, whether through a listening ear during tough times or through acts of kindness, the other is likely to reciprocate. This mutual exchange of care and support strengthens the relationship and encourages both partners to invest in the well-being of the other. Over time, this creates a virtuous cycle where both partners feel valued and supported, leading to lasting growth in the relationship. A couple that consistently practices trust and reciprocity is more likely to weather challenges together and come out stronger on the other side.

In business environments, trust and reciprocity are critical for building effective teams, forming strong client relationships, and driving organizational success. For example, a company that consistently delivers high-quality products and services on time fosters trust with its customers. This trust is reinforced when customers reciprocate by remaining loyal, referring others, or providing valuable feedback. As the business continues to deliver value, the cycle of trust and reciprocity strengthens, creating a loyal customer base and encouraging further growth. Likewise, within a workplace, when employees trust their managers and colleagues to act in their best interests, they are more likely to collaborate and contribute effectively. Managers who demonstrate transparency, provide opportunities for professional development, and recognize employees' efforts can encourage loyalty and motivation. In return, employees are more likely to reciprocate by being dedicated, taking initiative, and fostering a positive workplace culture. This cycle drives productivity, innovation, and overall growth, as employees and employers are more aligned in their goals and actions.

A well-functioning community, where trust is built through reciprocal actions, tends to experience less conflict, higher levels of cooperation, and more opportunities for social and economic growth. Similarly, in governance, when citizens trust their leaders to make decisions that benefit the public, they are more likely to support policies and participate in civic activities. Governments that cultivate trust by being transparent, responsive, and accountable to their citizens foster greater cooperation and a sense of shared purpose, leading to more effective governance and long-term societal growth.

However, the cultivation of trust and reciprocity is not always straightforward and requires attention to key factors such as transparency, consistency, and genuine intent. Trust is fragile, and any breach, whether intentional or accidental, can set back the cycle. For example, a company that fails to deliver on promises or a friend who repeatedly breaks trust can disrupt the process of reciprocity. In these situations, it is essential to rebuild trust through accountability, openness, and positive actions. Businesses can restore trust with customers by acknowledging mistakes and taking corrective measures, while individuals can restore personal relationships by being open about their actions and demonstrating commitment to making amends. When both parties are invested in the process of rebuilding and maintaining trust, reciprocity can be reestablished, and growth can continue.

In conclusion, cultivating trust and reciprocity is a powerful approach for ensuring lasting growth, whether in personal relationships, businesses, communities, or international relations. When individuals and groups invest in these principles, they create environments where cooperation thrives, opportunities multiply, and collective success becomes achievable. Trust forms the foundation of all meaningful interactions, while reciprocity ensures that these relationships are sustained and strengthened over time. By prioritizing trust and reciprocity in every aspect of life, people and organizations can foster long-term growth, resilience, and a sense of shared purpose that propels them toward continued success and fulfillment.

CHAPTER 6

The Role of Leadership in Sustaining the Cycle

Leadership plays a critical role in sustaining the cycle of trust and reciprocity, serving as the foundation for maintaining strong relationships, fostering collaboration, and driving long-term success. Effective leaders understand that trust is not a one-time achievement but an ongoing process that requires consistent effort, transparency, and positive reinforcement. By modeling behaviors that prioritize integrity, openness, and fairness, leaders can inspire trust and encourage reciprocal actions from their teams, organizations, or communities. When leaders demonstrate a commitment to the values of trust and reciprocity, they create an environment where cooperation and mutual respect thrive, leading to sustained growth and success.

For instance, in a corporate setting, a CEO who regularly communicates openly about the company's goals, challenges, and performance fosters transparency and trust among employees. When employees see their leader being transparent and honest, they are more likely to reciprocate with loyalty and commitment to the company's vision. This reciprocity helps to create a workplace culture where people are motivated to contribute their best efforts, collaborate across departments, and innovate without fear of being undermined or ignored. Additionally, a leader who recognizes and rewards employees for their contributions further strengthens the trust in the organization, as employees feel valued and motivated to continue working toward collective success.

In the realm of politics, a leader who consistently acts in the best interest of their citizens—by prioritizing ethical governance, listening to diverse perspectives, and delivering on promises—creates a cycle of trust and reciprocity with the public. For example, when a leader takes responsibility for their actions and makes efforts to address the needs of the community, citizens are more likely to support policies and engage in civic duties. This trust, once established, becomes the foundation for continued collaboration, with citizens reciprocating by participating in social programs, voting, and working together to improve their society.

Similarly, in education, a teacher who demonstrates trustworthiness and fairness in their interactions with students can cultivate a learning environment that encourages respect, responsibility, and collaboration. When students trust their teacher, they are more likely to reciprocate by engaging with the material, respecting the classroom rules, and offering support to their peers. This reciprocal relationship between teacher and student creates an atmosphere where both parties are invested in each other's growth and success, enhancing the overall educational experience.

In all these examples, leadership is about more than just making decisions; it is about creating an environment where trust is consistently nurtured and where reciprocal actions lead to long-term growth. Leaders who understand the importance of trust and reciprocity can sustain positive cycles that benefit individuals, teams, organizations, and societies as a whole.

Leadership as Service

Leadership as service is a concept that redefines traditional views of leadership by focusing on the leader's role in supporting others rather than seeking power or personal gain. In this approach, leaders prioritize the well-being and growth of those they lead, fostering an environment where collaboration, empowerment, and mutual respect thrive. Leaders who adopt this mindset recognize that their success is tied to the success of their teams or communities, and they serve as facilitators, helping others achieve their full potential. Through empathy, humility, and a genuine commitment to others, service-oriented leaders build trust, create positive cultures, and drive long-term success.

For instance, in a corporate setting, a leader who regularly communicates openly about company goals, challenges, and progress fosters transparency and trust among employees. When employees see their leader being honest and clear, they are more likely to reciprocate with loyalty, engagement, and a commitment to the organization's success.

This reciprocity helps create a workplace culture where collaboration is encouraged, individuals are motivated to contribute their best efforts, and the organization grows as a result. In this way, the leader's focus on service to others strengthens both individual and collective achievements.

In education, a teacher who goes above and beyond to meet students' needs is another example of leadership as service. Teachers who offer extra help, create inclusive environments, and listen to their students contribute to a positive and supportive learning atmosphere. When students feel that their teacher genuinely cares about their success, they are more likely to engage with the material, follow the guidance provided, and contribute to the overall classroom culture. This reciprocal relationship helps to build trust between the teacher and students, fostering an environment where learning and growth are prioritized.

In health care, leaders in caregiving roles, such as doctors or nurses, demonstrate leadership as service by advocating for their patients' care and well-being. By offering compassion, attentiveness, and dedicated service, health care professionals create a sense of trust with their patients, who then feel comfortable engaging in their treatment and following advice. When health care providers consistently place the needs of patients first, they not only improve individual health outcomes but also contribute to the overall quality of care in the community.

In nonprofit organizations, leadership as service becomes particularly apparent as the leader's focus shifts from profit to service to others. A leader in this sector often dedicates their time and resources to addressing social issues and improving the lives of disadvantaged individuals or communities. By putting the mission before personal gain, they foster trust among donors, volunteers, and the communities they serve. Their example of selfless service inspires others to get involved, creating a ripple effect of giving and support that strengthens the organization's efforts and leads to meaningful change.

One of the key aspects of leadership as service is the empowerment of others. Service-oriented leaders recognize that their role is not to control or direct every aspect of the process, but to equip others with the tools, resources, and support they need to succeed. In a workplace, for example, a leader who provides employees with autonomy, encourages professional development, and creates opportunities for growth is practicing leadership as service. Employees who feel empowered are more likely to take ownership of their roles, contribute their skills, and collaborate effectively, leading to greater productivity and job satisfaction.

Ultimately, leadership as service is about focusing on the growth, well-being, and success of others. Leaders who embody this mindset create environments where people feel supported, valued, and motivated to contribute to collective success. Whether in business, education, health care, or social causes, service-oriented leadership helps build a strong foundation of trust and collaboration. By serving the needs of others, leaders inspire those around them to reach their full potential, leading to lasting, positive change and sustainable growth. In this way, leadership becomes a powerful tool for creating a cycle of growth, empowerment, and mutual respect that benefits everyone involved.

Modeling Trust and Reciprocity

Modeling trust and reciprocity is a powerful way for leaders, organizations, and individuals to establish and reinforce the foundations of positive relationships and sustainable growth. When leaders and individuals actively demonstrate trustworthiness and engage in reciprocal actions, they set a powerful example that encourages others to follow suit. Trust is built over time through consistent actions, and reciprocity strengthens the bonds between people by creating an environment where mutual respect, cooperation, and goodwill flourish. By modeling these behaviors, leaders not only inspire those around them to trust and support one another, but they also create a culture where these values are continuously reinforced, leading to long-term success and collaboration.

A key example of modeling trust and reciprocity can be found in the relationship between managers and employees. When a manager demonstrates trust by empowering employees with responsibility and autonomy, it signals confidence in their abilities. This trust allows employees to feel respected and valued, which in turn motivates them to reciprocate with higher levels of commitment, effort, and loyalty to the organization. For instance, when a manager shares important information about the company's challenges and future plans, it builds transparency and trust. Employees who feel trusted with such information are more likely to reciprocate by being open about their concerns and contributing to finding solutions. This creates a cycle of trust and reciprocity, where both parties contribute to each other's success.

In teams, trust and reciprocity can be modeled through collaboration and shared responsibility. A team leader who demonstrates trust by delegating important tasks and recognizing the skills and expertise of team members sets a positive example for the group. When team members feel trusted to contribute their unique strengths, they are more likely to reciprocate by actively supporting each other, sharing knowledge, and helping one another to achieve common goals. For example, a project manager who trusts their team to handle critical components of a project and acknowledges their contributions fosters a sense of ownership and accountability within the team. As a result, the team members are more likely to go above and beyond to ensure the success of the project, knowing that their efforts are appreciated and valued.

In the context of community leadership, trust and reciprocity can be modeled by those in positions of authority who serve the public interest. Community leaders who are transparent about their goals and actions, and who prioritize the well-being of the community, set an example for others to follow. When residents see that their leaders act with integrity and fairness, they are more likely to reciprocate by participating in community activities, volunteering, and supporting initiatives that benefit the group. For example, if a local leader listens to the concerns of the community, takes action to address those concerns, and follows through on promises, the community will likely reciprocate by supporting that leader in future efforts, creating a cycle of trust and collaboration.

In education, teachers who model trust and reciprocity in the classroom create an environment where students feel safe, valued, and motivated to contribute. For instance, a teacher who trusts students to take ownership of their learning by offering them opportunities to make decisions and express their opinions demonstrates confidence in their abilities. When students feel trusted, they are more likely to reciprocate by taking their learning seriously, participating actively in class discussions, and helping their peers. This reciprocal relationship fosters a sense of responsibility and respect, creating a positive learning environment where both the teacher and the students thrive.

In family dynamics, parents can model trust and reciprocity by encouraging open communication, demonstrating fairness, and leading by example. When a parent shows trust in their child by giving them responsibilities and involving them in family decisions, it helps to build a relationship of mutual respect. The child, in turn, is more likely to reciprocate by taking those responsibilities seriously, contributing to family tasks, and supporting the parents when needed. This creates a balanced relationship where both parties feel valued and respected, leading to stronger family bonds and a more harmonious home environment.

By modeling trust and reciprocity, leaders and individuals inspire others to adopt similar behaviors, creating a positive feedback loop that strengthens relationships and encourages long-term growth. In any setting, whether in the workplace, community, family, or friendships, when people see others acting with trust and reciprocating positive actions, they are more likely to follow suit. This cycle not only fosters a culture of mutual respect but also leads to increased collaboration, deeper connections, and greater success for all involved. Trust and reciprocity, when consistently modeled and nurtured, become the cornerstone of healthy, thriving relationships and communities.

Creating a Culture of Growth

Creating a culture of growth is essential for fostering continuous improvement, innovation, and success within any organization or community. A culture of growth goes beyond individual development and focuses on nurturing an environment where both people and processes evolve over time. In such a culture, learning is encouraged, challenges are seen as opportunities for development, and individuals are empowered to contribute their ideas and strengths. Leaders play a crucial role in shaping and maintaining this culture by modeling behaviors that prioritize growth, offering support and resources for learning, and celebrating achievements while encouraging further progress.

One of the foundational elements of a culture of growth is the belief in the potential for development. For example, in a workplace, leaders who provide opportunities for employees to grow professionally, whether through training programs, mentorship, or exposure to new challenges, send a powerful message that development is a core value. When employees see that their personal growth is supported, they are more likely to invest in their own learning and development. This commitment to growth can lead to improved skills, higher job satisfaction, and greater innovation, as employees are more confident in their abilities and feel equipped to contribute meaningfully to the organization's goals. For instance, a company that invests in ongoing professional development or provides career progression opportunities helps to cultivate a workforce that is adaptable, knowledgeable, and motivated to improve.

In educational settings, a culture of growth encourages both teachers and students to view learning as a continuous journey. When teachers create a classroom environment where mistakes are seen as learning opportunities and effort is valued over perfection, they help students develop a growth mindset. This mindset, which emphasizes that abilities can be developed through dedication and hard work, leads to increased resilience, creativity, and a willingness to take on challenges. For example, a teacher who encourages students to engage with new ideas and provides constructive feedback rather than simply grading their work fosters a culture of intellectual curiosity and growth. In turn, students become more open to learning and are more likely to pursue their academic goals with a sense of purpose and motivation.

Similarly, in sports teams, a culture of growth is critical to the development of athletes and the success of the team. Coaches who emphasize effort, teamwork, and improvement rather than just the end result create an environment where players feel supported and motivated to continuously improve their skills. For example, a coach who acknowledges individual progress, whether in terms of technique or mental resilience, helps players to stay focused on their own growth. This approach encourages athletes to view setbacks as part of their learning process rather than failures, leading to higher performance levels and greater team cohesion. When athletes believe that they are part of a team that values growth, they are more likely to push themselves to develop further.

In a community or social context, creating a culture of growth involves fostering a spirit of collaboration and shared purpose. For example, a community that encourages volunteerism, open dialogue, and mutual support creates an environment where individuals feel empowered to contribute to the common good. A leader in such a community may actively seek out and support individuals who are passionate about making a positive impact, helping them to grow and develop their own skills and leadership potential. In this way, a culture of growth can strengthen the community as a whole, allowing members to work together toward shared goals while simultaneously nurturing their individual talents and capacities. For example, a local nonprofit organization that invests in training its volunteers not only boosts the skills of the individuals but also enhances the effectiveness of the entire organization in addressing community needs.

A culture of growth also requires a commitment to feedback and reflection. Regular feedback, both positive and constructive, helps individuals and teams recognize areas of strength and identify opportunities for improvement. For example, in a team setting, a leader who provides specific, actionable feedback after each project encourages team members to reflect on their performance and identify ways to improve in the future. This culture of feedback helps to create an environment where people are constantly learning and growing, rather than stagnating in their roles. When feedback is given in a supportive manner and is seen as an opportunity for development rather than criticism, it promotes a sense of trust and openness within the team, which is essential for ongoing growth.

In family environments, a culture of growth can be nurtured by encouraging open communication, supporting individual goals, and creating a home life that values continuous learning. Parents who encourage their children to explore new interests, take on new challenges, and learn from their experiences foster a mindset of growth that can extend into adulthood. For example, parents who praise their children's efforts in trying new things, rather than just their achievements, help them develop resilience and a positive attitude toward failure. This creates a family culture where personal growth is prioritized, and each family member feels supported in their journey of self-improvement.

In conclusion, creating a culture of growth involves cultivating an environment where learning, development, and improvement are valued and supported. Whether in the workplace, classroom, sports, community, or family, a growth-oriented culture fosters a sense of empowerment and continuous progress. By encouraging individuals to take risks, learn from their mistakes, and pursue their potential, organizations and communities can unlock greater creativity, collaboration, and success. In this type of culture, growth becomes a shared value, driving both personal and collective achievements and contributing to long-term, sustainable progress.

Nurturing the *Give–Get–Grow* Cycle Through Leadership

Nurturing the *give–get–grow* cycle through leadership involves creating an environment where both leaders and followers contribute in meaningful ways, resulting in mutual benefits that lead to collective growth. Leaders play a pivotal role in setting the tone for this cycle by modeling behaviors that emphasize generosity, trust, and collaboration. When leaders actively give their time, resources, and support to their teams or communities, they create a sense of security and goodwill, encouraging others to reciprocate. This reciprocity leads to the growth of both the individuals involved and the organization as a whole, creating a positive feedback loop that continually reinforces itself.

An example of nurturing the *give–get–grow* cycle can be seen in the way leaders provide opportunities for professional development. A leader who invests in training programs or mentorship for their team members is essentially giving valuable resources to support their growth. In return, employees who feel supported and equipped with new skills are more likely to contribute more effectively to the organization. They may take on more responsibility, offer innovative ideas, or mentor others in turn, thus contributing to the overall growth of the organization. This cycle not only benefits individual employees but also strengthens the entire organization by cultivating a culture of continuous learning and improvement.

In the context of education, teachers often nurture this cycle by giving their time and expertise to their students, creating an environment that fosters growth. A teacher who provides individualized attention, encourages critical thinking, and creates opportunities for students to express themselves is giving a significant amount of support to their students' intellectual and personal development. In response, students are likely to engage more actively in their learning, demonstrate improved performance, and contribute positively to the classroom environment. As students grow and develop, they are able to give back to the teacher by participating more fully in class activities, sharing ideas with their peers, and contributing to the learning culture. This cycle not only helps students succeed academically but also cultivates a deeper sense of mutual respect and trust between teachers and students.

In a community setting, leaders who model generosity and care for the well-being of others nurture a *give–get–grow* cycle that strengthens the social fabric. For example, a community leader who volunteers time to organize events, address local issues, or support individuals in need sets an example for others. The act of giving selflessly motivates others in the community to get involved and contribute, whether through volunteering, sharing resources, or helping neighbors. As more people get involved, the community grows stronger, and the leader's initial act of giving inspires further generosity. This positive cycle creates a culture of service, where members are more connected, supportive of one another, and committed to collective progress.

In family dynamics, parents can nurture the *give–get–grow* cycle by offering support, guidance, and love while encouraging their children to reciprocate by taking responsibility for their actions and contributing to the family unit. Parents who model respect, empathy, and hard work show their children how to be responsible and considerate individuals. Children, in turn, learn the value of contributing to family responsibilities, helping others, and growing into compassionate and capable individuals. This cycle of giving and receiving not only strengthens the bond between parents and children but also instills values that support the child's future growth and success in life. As children grow, they are likely to give back to their parents by becoming independent and successful, creating a lasting cycle of mutual care and respect.

A strong example of nurturing the *give–get–grow* cycle can be seen in the relationship between mentors and mentees. A mentor who invests time in sharing knowledge, offering advice, and providing guidance is giving invaluable support to the mentee's personal and professional development. In response, the mentee's growth and success serve as a testament to the mentor's efforts. Over time, as the mentee becomes more capable, they may choose to give back by mentoring others, thus continuing the cycle. This process not only benefits the individuals involved but also contributes to a broader culture of support and shared knowledge within an organization or community. The mentor's initial giving creates a ripple effect of growth that spreads beyond just the mentee.

Leaders in health care can also play a crucial role in nurturing the *give–get–grow* cycle. A doctor or nurse who demonstrates empathy and dedicates time to their patients' care is giving a valuable service to the community. In response, patients who feel genuinely cared for and respected are more likely to follow medical advice, adopt healthier lifestyles, and contribute positively to their own health outcomes. As patients grow healthier, they often become advocates for health care, supporting and encouraging others to seek care. This cycle creates an environment where trust, care, and mutual benefit are shared by both health care providers and patients, leading to improved outcomes and stronger community health.

In conclusion, nurturing the *give–get–grow* cycle through leadership is about creating a dynamic environment where trust, reciprocity, and mutual respect are fundamental values. Whether in business, education, health care, or family, leaders who model generosity, invest in others' growth, and foster a culture of collaboration and support create an ongoing cycle of improvement. As individuals grow through the support they receive, they are more likely to give back, contributing to the growth of others and the broader community. This cycle of giving, receiving, and growing leads to sustainable success, stronger relationships, and a continuous positive impact on both individuals and organizations.

Leadership as the Catalyst for Collective Growth

Leadership acts as the catalyst for collective growth by creating environments where individuals feel empowered, supported, and motivated to contribute their best efforts for the greater good. When leaders embrace their role as facilitators of growth, they set in motion a cycle where the development of individuals leads to the overall advancement of teams, organizations, and communities. Through guidance, inspiration, and a commitment to the well-being of others, leaders can unlock potential, drive innovation, and foster collaboration that collectively propels everyone forward. Leadership is not just about directing or managing; it is about inspiring others to reach new heights while working together toward shared goals.

In a business context, effective leadership can transform an organization by aligning individual growth with the company's larger objectives. For example, a business leader who invests in leadership development programs and creates opportunities for employees to learn new skills does more than just improve individual performance. By fostering a culture where employees feel valued and have room to grow, the leader simultaneously strengthens the organization. As employees develop new capabilities, they contribute more effectively, boosting innovation, productivity, and company success. This mutually beneficial relationship not only helps the organization thrive but also promotes employee satisfaction and loyalty, further reinforcing the cycle of growth.

Similarly, in the education system, leaders who champion innovation, collaboration, and continuous learning can have a profound impact on both teachers and students. When a school principal encourages teachers to experiment with new teaching methods and provides professional development opportunities, it supports educators in their own growth. In turn, the teachers pass on their newfound knowledge and improved practices to students, enhancing the learning experience. This creates a ripple effect that elevates the entire educational environment. Teachers who feel supported and empowered are more likely to foster a growth mindset in their students, encouraging them to engage in their education and achieve greater academic success. In this way, leadership in education acts as a catalyst for collective growth, benefiting not only the staff but also the students and the community as a whole.

In the realm of community leadership, leaders who prioritize the collective well-being of their communities foster an environment where people feel connected, supported, and motivated to contribute to shared goals. A community leader who organizes programs to address local needs, engages in transparent communication, and encourages volunteerism fosters a sense of ownership and responsibility among community members. As individuals work together on projects and initiatives, they not only improve their immediate surroundings but also strengthen the community's social fabric. This collaborative spirit helps to create a cycle of giving, where individuals invest in each other's growth, resulting in a stronger, more resilient community. Leadership in this context serves as the catalyst that brings people together, turning individual efforts into a collective movement for progress.

In the health care sector, leadership can be a powerful driver of collective growth by focusing on both patient care and the development of health care professionals. Leaders in health care settings who prioritize training, well-being, and support for their staff ensure that doctors, nurses, and other health care professionals are equipped to provide high-quality care. As these professionals grow in their roles, they are better able to serve their patients, leading to improved health outcomes. This growth in individual capabilities and care translates into broader improvements in the health care system, where more people benefit from enhanced services. Leaders who model compassionate care, foster collaboration among teams, and support professional development create a positive feedback loop where both providers and patients grow together.

At its core, leadership as the catalyst for collective growth is about recognizing that the success of a group or organization is deeply intertwined with the growth of its individuals. Whether in business, education, sports, health care, or communities, effective leaders understand that empowering others and creating opportunities for personal development leads to a more robust and resilient collective. When leaders invest in others' growth and create an environment where learning and collaboration are valued, they cultivate a culture that benefits everyone involved. This culture of growth not only drives the immediate success of teams and organizations but also lays the foundation for long-term, sustainable progress. Leadership, when executed with an emphasis on growth and development, fosters a cycle where individuals and groups evolve together, achieving greater success collectively.

CHAPTER 7

Building and Maintaining Resilient Communities

Building and maintaining resilient communities is essential for creating environments that can withstand challenges, adapt to change, and continue to thrive in the face of adversity. Resilience in a community is not only about recovering from difficult situations but also about fostering a collective strength that enables individuals to support one another, adapt to evolving circumstances, and work together toward shared goals. Leaders play a crucial role in this process by promoting a culture of cooperation, mutual support, and proactive problem-solving. However, the responsibility for resilience extends beyond leaders to every member of the community, as everyone plays a part in strengthening the bonds that hold the community together.

One key aspect of building resilient communities is promoting strong social connections and support networks. When community members know and trust one another, they are better able to collaborate and help each other in times of need. For example, during natural disasters such as hurricanes or floods, communities with strong ties often see neighbors helping one another with resources, shelter, or emotional support. This network of support fosters a sense of belonging and shared responsibility, making it easier for people to navigate tough times together. In such communities, resilience is not solely dependent on external aid or recovery programs; rather, it comes from the internal strength of the relationships that have been built over time.

Education is another critical element in building community resilience. By investing in educational initiatives, communities can empower individuals with the knowledge, skills, and resources they need to navigate challenges effectively. For instance, programs that teach practical skills such as financial literacy, conflict resolution, or first aid can prepare community members to respond to both everyday and crisis situations. Additionally, educating young people about sustainability, social responsibility, and resilience helps to instill values that promote long-term community well-being. When individuals are equipped with the tools to solve problems, make informed decisions, and support one another, they contribute to a community that can adapt and grow, even in the face of adversity.

Economic resilience is equally important for maintaining strong communities. Communities with diverse and sustainable economies are better able to weather economic downturns, job losses, or market disruptions. For example, communities that encourage local entrepreneurship, support small businesses, and promote skill development can build a robust local economy that provides stability. When local businesses thrive, they not only contribute to economic growth but also foster a sense of pride and ownership among community members. Additionally, job training programs and initiatives that help individuals transition into new industries can improve the overall adaptability of the workforce. This approach ensures that the community is not overly reliant on a single industry or employer, making it more resilient to economic shifts.

A crucial part of maintaining resilient communities is fostering inclusivity and ensuring that everyone has a voice in community decision making. Inclusive communities are stronger because they bring together diverse perspectives, ideas, and solutions to problems. For example, communities that actively involve underrepresented groups in discussions about local policies, infrastructure, and community projects are more likely to create solutions that meet the needs of everyone. These communities are better equipped to handle social challenges, such as inequality or discrimination, because they prioritize collaboration and understanding. Moreover, inclusivity strengthens the social fabric, as people feel valued and empowered to contribute to the collective well-being of the community.

Mental and emotional resilience also plays a significant role in a community's ability to maintain its strength during difficult times. Support systems such as counseling services, peer groups, and mental health resources can help individuals cope with the stresses and trauma that arise during crises. For example, after a natural disaster or personal loss, communities with strong mental health support networks are better equipped to help individuals process their emotions and rebuild their lives. Leaders within these communities who prioritize mental well-being and encourage open dialogue about mental health challenges contribute to an environment where people feel safe seeking help. This emotional resilience ensures that community members do not face adversity alone and can heal together as a collective.

Building resilient communities also involves fostering a sense of shared purpose and collective responsibility. When people feel connected to a common goal, they are more likely to invest in the community's success. For instance, in neighborhoods where residents take pride in maintaining local parks, organizing cleanup efforts, or supporting local initiatives, there is a shared sense of ownership and accountability. This collective action not only enhances the physical environment but also strengthens the bonds between community members. Shared responsibility encourages individuals to take initiative, solve problems together, and build a sense of pride in their community's accomplishments.

In conclusion, building and maintaining resilient communities requires a multifaceted approach that encompasses social connection, education, economic stability, inclusivity, infrastructure, and mental well-being. When community members feel supported, equipped, and engaged, they are better able to face challenges together and ensure that their community not only survives but thrives. Leadership is critical in creating a vision for resilience and empowering individuals to contribute to collective growth, but it is the active participation of all community members that sustains this resilience over time. By fostering collaboration, planning for the future, and supporting each other through both everyday challenges and crises, communities can create a foundation that ensures long-term strength and adaptability.

What Makes a Community Resilient?

A resilient community is one that can withstand and adapt to challenges, whether they are economic, social, environmental, or political. The core qualities that make a community resilient include strong social networks, the ability to innovate, economic stability, and the presence of supportive leadership. These elements allow a community not only to recover from adversity but also to emerge stronger and more cohesive. Resilience in a community is built over time through collective effort, planning, and a focus on both immediate recovery and long-term sustainability.

One of the primary factors that contribute to a community's resilience is its social fabric. Strong social networks provide individuals with a sense of belonging and mutual support, which are vital during times of crisis. For example, during the COVID-19 pandemic, many communities with tight-knit social connections saw neighbors helping each other by delivering groceries, offering childcare, or providing emotional support. These social ties allow people to weather challenges more effectively because they know they can rely on others. Additionally, when people feel connected to one another, they are more likely to engage in collaborative efforts, strengthening the community's collective ability to adapt and thrive. These networks foster trust and ensure that individuals are not isolated during difficult times.

Economic stability and diversity also contribute to a community's resilience. Communities that rely on a single industry or employer are more vulnerable to economic shifts, but those with diverse sources of income tend to weather downturns better. For example, a town dependent on mining may struggle if the industry collapses, whereas a town that has developed a mix of agriculture, tourism, and technology-based businesses has multiple avenues for economic growth. A community that fosters entrepreneurship and small business development is also more resilient because it allows individuals to create jobs, support local commerce, and reduce dependency on outside sources of employment. By nurturing economic diversity, communities can better absorb shocks and remain self-sufficient during tough times.

Inclusive leadership is also essential for fostering a resilient community. Leaders who engage with and listen to all members of the community—regardless of race, class, or background—are better positioned to guide the community through difficult situations. Inclusive leadership ensures that everyone's needs are addressed and that no one is left behind. For example, in times of crisis, a leader who makes an effort to reach out to marginalized groups can help ensure they have access to resources such as food, shelter, and health care. By prioritizing inclusivity, leaders can unite the community around shared goals, making the collective response to a crisis stronger and more effective.

Finally, the presence of mental and emotional resilience is a crucial element that contributes to the strength of a community. Communities that prioritize mental health and offer support systems, such as counseling, peer support groups, and community centers, are more resilient during times of stress. For instance, after a traumatic event like a natural disaster or mass tragedy, communities with access to mental health resources tend to recover more quickly because individuals have the support they need to process their emotions. When people feel emotionally supported, they are better able to cope with stress and adversity, which in turn helps the community move forward together.

In conclusion, a resilient community is one that is built on strong social connections, innovation, economic stability, preparedness, inclusive leadership, and mental health support. These factors enable a community to not only endure challenges but also grow from them. Communities that invest in these elements are more likely to recover from adversity and emerge stronger, with improved systems, better resources, and a greater sense of unity. The ability to adapt, collaborate, and innovate in the face of challenges is what truly defines a resilient community, allowing it to thrive in an ever-changing world.

The Role of Connection and Collaboration in Building Resilience

The role of connection and collaboration in building resilience is central to ensuring that communities, organizations, and individuals can withstand challenges and emerge stronger from adversity. When people are connected to one another and collaborate effectively, they can pool resources, share knowledge, and provide emotional support, all of which are essential for navigating difficult times. Connection fosters a sense of belonging and solidarity, while collaboration allows for the collective intelligence and creativity needed to solve problems and adapt to changing circumstances. Together, these elements form the backbone of resilience, helping individuals and communities thrive in the face of uncertainty.

Connection is fundamental to building resilience because it creates a support network that individuals can rely on during times of stress or crisis. In communities with strong social bonds, people are more likely to offer help and support one another when challenges arise. For instance, during natural disasters such as earthquakes or floods, communities that have established networks of mutual aid tend to recover more quickly. Neighbors may share food, provide temporary shelter, or assist with repairs. In a tight-knit community, the shared sense of responsibility and connection ensures that no one faces hardship alone, and people are more likely to rally together to help those in need. This support system makes the community stronger by enabling individuals to overcome adversity with the help of others.

Collaboration enhances resilience by enabling diverse perspectives and skills to come together in problem-solving. When people collaborate, they can generate more innovative solutions to challenges. For example, in response to the COVID-19 pandemic, many health care organizations, governments, and nonprofit groups collaborated across sectors to distribute vaccines, share vital medical supplies, and provide financial assistance to individuals affected by the crisis. This level of collaboration ensured that resources were used efficiently and that more people received the help they needed, resulting in faster recovery and greater collective strength. Collaboration within teams, businesses, or communities enables a pooling of resources and expertise, which not only helps to address immediate challenges but also builds capacity for future resilience.

Education and schools also benefit from connection and collaboration in fostering resilience. Teachers, students, parents, and communities working together can create a learning environment that is adaptable, supportive, and responsive to the needs of all involved. For example, during the shift to online learning due to the pandemic, many schools relied on collaboration between teachers, parents, and students to overcome technological and logistical challenges. Parents supported their children at home by providing a stable environment for online lessons, while teachers adapted their teaching methods to suit virtual formats. School administrators worked with local communities to ensure that families had access to the necessary technology and resources. This collective effort allowed students to continue their education despite the challenges, and it highlighted the importance of connection and collaboration in overcoming obstacles.

Furthermore, in the context of environmental resilience, collaboration is key to addressing global challenges such as climate change. Communities, businesses, and governments that collaborate to develop sustainable practices and policies can create a collective response to environmental issues that is far more impactful than individual efforts alone. For example, coastal communities that work together with environmental organizations and governmental agencies to implement coastal protection measures, such as mangrove restoration or sustainable tourism practices, help to safeguard their local ecosystems while also protecting their livelihoods. Through collaboration, communities can share knowledge, resources, and strategies that help them adapt to environmental changes and reduce their vulnerability to future crises.

In conclusion, connection and collaboration are vital components of building resilience at both the individual and community levels. Strong social ties create support networks that help people navigate crises, while collaboration brings together diverse skills and perspectives to generate innovative solutions. Whether in response to natural disasters, economic challenges, social issues, or personal struggles, communities that prioritize connection and collaboration are better equipped to adapt, recover, and grow. By fostering a culture of mutual support and collective problem-solving, communities can build lasting resilience that enables them to thrive in the face of adversity.

Communication: The Lifeblood of Resilience

Communication is the lifeblood of resilience, serving as the foundation for building trust, coordinating efforts, and maintaining a sense of community during times of crisis or adversity. Effective communication allows individuals and groups to share information, align their actions, and support one another. In times of uncertainty, clear and consistent communication can make the difference between confusion and coordinated action. It enables communities, organizations, and individuals to respond to challenges more effectively, fostering collaboration and problem-solving while minimizing the risks of misunderstanding and fragmentation.

One of the key aspects of communication that contributes to resilience is transparency. When leaders and organizations communicate openly about challenges, expectations, and progress, they build trust and ensure that everyone is on the same page. For example, during the COVID-19 pandemic, governments and health organizations that provided regular, honest updates on the status of the virus, preventive measures, and vaccination efforts helped to reduce fear and confusion. Communities that received clear information about safety protocols were better able to protect themselves and their loved ones. In contrast, a lack of communication or misinformation can create fear, uncertainty, and even resistance to necessary actions, undermining resilience. Transparent communication fosters a sense of security and unity, helping communities and organizations work together to overcome adversity.

Another critical role of communication in resilience is in coordinating efforts. Whether it's a community responding to a natural disaster or an organization dealing with an economic crisis, effective communication ensures that resources are allocated efficiently, and efforts are synchronized. For example, in the aftermath of a major earthquake, emergency response teams rely on communication to assess the damage, deploy resources, and provide aid to those in need. Local officials must relay critical information about areas that need attention, while volunteers and aid organizations must coordinate their efforts to prevent duplication of resources. In this context, communication allows for a rapid, organized response, ensuring that every part of the affected community receives the support it requires. Without clear and continuous communication, the response can become chaotic and less effective, prolonging the recovery process.

In organizations, internal communication is essential for maintaining a resilient workforce. During periods of change or crisis, employees look to their leaders for guidance, reassurance, and clarity about the future. A company that maintains open lines of communication with its staff—whether through regular meetings, updates, or feedback sessions—can help employees feel supported and involved in the organization's response to challenges. For example, during the financial crisis of 2008, many businesses that kept their employees informed about the company's status, potential layoffs, and strategies for recovery were able to maintain higher levels of employee morale and loyalty. Transparent and empathetic communication during times of hardship allows employees to feel valued, reducing uncertainty and helping to maintain their commitment to the organization.

Communication also plays a pivotal role in maintaining social connections, which are crucial for building personal and community resilience. When individuals feel connected to others, they are more likely to overcome personal challenges and contribute to the collective strength of the community. For instance, during the pandemic, many people used video calls, social media, and phone conversations to stay in touch with family and friends, even when physical distance was required. These forms of communication allowed individuals to continue supporting one another emotionally, reducing feelings of isolation and loneliness. In communities, effective communication also facilitates the sharing of resources, such as food drives, volunteer efforts, and local services, which can make a significant difference in times of need. People who feel connected are more likely to engage in collaborative efforts that strengthen the community and contribute to collective resilience.

Moreover, communication can serve as a tool for empowerment. In resilient communities, people are encouraged to voice their concerns, share their experiences, and contribute their ideas to solve problems. When individuals feel heard and understood, they are more likely to take proactive steps to address challenges and support others. For example, in community organizing efforts aimed at social justice or local environmental initiatives, communication allows diverse voices to be heard and collective action to take place. By facilitating discussions and providing platforms for individuals to express themselves, leaders can foster a sense of ownership and agency, empowering community members to take action and advocate for positive change.

Lastly, the role of communication in resilience extends to fostering a culture of learning and adaptation. In resilient organizations and communities, there is a constant flow of feedback, both from leaders to members and among peers, that helps to identify areas for improvement and respond to emerging challenges. For example, in the workplace, organizations that encourage open communication channels for feedback can learn from mistakes, adjust strategies, and innovate to overcome obstacles. In communities, effective communication can ensure that lessons learned from past experiences—such as disaster response or community development projects—are shared and applied to future efforts. By creating a culture of ongoing communication, communities and organizations can continuously evolve, strengthening their ability to cope with future challenges.

In conclusion, communication is fundamental to building and sustaining resilience. It fosters trust, ensures coordination, connects people, and empowers individuals to contribute to collective efforts. Transparent, timely, and empathetic communication helps to manage uncertainty, reduce stress, and create a sense of shared purpose. Whether in the context of personal challenges, organizational change, or community crises, communication enables people to adapt, collaborate, and persevere. By prioritizing effective communication, individuals, organizations, and communities can enhance their resilience, emerging stronger and more united in every aspect.

Preparing for Adversity: Building a Resilient Mindset

Preparing for adversity is a key aspect of building resilience, and one of the most effective ways to navigate life's challenges is by cultivating a resilient mindset. A resilient mindset involves embracing change, staying positive in the face of difficulties, and being proactive in addressing problems before they escalate. It is about developing the mental and emotional tools to cope with setbacks, learn from failures, and continue moving forward. This mindset can be developed through intentional practices such as building emotional awareness, focusing on solutions, and fostering a growth-oriented attitude.

One of the foundational elements of a resilient mindset is the ability to reframe negative experiences. People with resilient mindsets don't view challenges as insurmountable obstacles but as opportunities for growth and learning. For example, consider an individual who faces a setback in their career, such as being passed over for a promotion. Instead of internalizing the failure and seeing it as a reflection of their worth, a resilient person would view it as a chance to reassess their strengths, identify areas for improvement, and focus on preparing for future opportunities. This ability to reframe challenges enables individuals to recover from setbacks more quickly and continue to strive toward their goals. It helps prevent the feeling of helplessness that can arise from adversity and empowers individuals to take control of their response to difficulties.

Another key component of a resilient mindset is emotional regulation. Resilience is not about avoiding negative emotions but about managing them effectively when they arise. People with resilient mindsets understand that stress, frustration, and disappointment are natural reactions to adversity, but they don't allow these emotions to dictate their behavior or derail their progress. For example, in the wake of a personal crisis, such as the loss of a loved one, an individual with a resilient mindset may experience sadness and grief but also recognize the importance of taking care of their well-being and continuing to engage with their community. They might seek support from friends or engage in activities that bring them peace, such as exercise or meditation. By acknowledging their emotions and using healthy coping mechanisms, individuals can maintain emotional balance and prevent overwhelming feelings from hindering their recovery.

Proactivity is also a cornerstone of building a resilient mindset. Resilient individuals don't wait for adversity to strike before taking action; they anticipate challenges and prepare for them in advance. For instance, a business leader who anticipates economic downturns might put measures in place to safeguard the company's financial health, such as diversifying income streams or reducing costs before the crisis hits. Similarly, someone preparing for a major life change, such as moving to a new city or changing careers, can build resilience by learning new skills, strengthening their social networks, and researching potential challenges ahead of time. By preparing in advance, individuals are better equipped to handle the unknown and can approach adversity with a sense of confidence and readiness.

A resilient mindset also involves cultivating a sense of optimism, even in the face of difficulty. While this does not mean ignoring the reality of tough situations, it involves focusing on the potential for positive outcomes. A resilient person maintains hope and believes that things can improve with effort, time, and perseverance. For example, in the aftermath of a natural disaster, a community that has experienced widespread destruction might face significant rebuilding challenges. However, if the community remains optimistic and focused on recovery—through collaborative efforts and planning for a better, safer future—they are more likely to succeed in restoring their homes and livelihoods. Optimism fuels the energy needed to overcome setbacks, and it encourages individuals and groups to keep moving forward, even when the path ahead seems difficult.

Support systems also play a crucial role in developing a resilient mindset. No one can face adversity alone, and resilient individuals recognize the importance of leaning on others for support. Building and maintaining strong personal networks—whether through family, friends, mentors, or colleagues—creates a safety net during challenging times. For instance, a person going through a major health issue may rely on their family and friends for emotional and practical support, whether it's providing meals, helping with childcare, or simply offering a listening ear. In this way, resilient individuals recognize that seeking support is not a sign of weakness but a necessary step in navigating challenges. By cultivating supportive relationships, individuals can bolster their emotional resources, making it easier to weather difficult times.

A growth-oriented mindset is another important aspect of resilience. Instead of seeing challenges as roadblocks, individuals with a growth mindset view them as opportunities to develop new skills, gain experience, and become stronger. For example, someone who faces a series of failed business ventures might use each setback as a lesson, analyzing what went wrong and finding ways to improve for the next attempt. They understand that failure is not a permanent condition but a temporary setback on the path to success. This mindset fosters perseverance and adaptability, qualities that are essential for bouncing back from adversity. By focusing on growth and improvement, individuals are more likely to persist through challenges, knowing that each experience, even the difficult ones, adds to their personal growth.

In conclusion, preparing for adversity by building a resilient mindset is essential for navigating life's inevitable challenges. By cultivating emotional regulation, proactivity, optimism, and a growth-oriented attitude, individuals can face setbacks with greater strength and determination. A resilient mindset enables people to recover from adversity, learn from experiences, and continue to grow. Additionally, support systems and community resources play a crucial role in building resilience, as they provide the encouragement and practical help needed during difficult times. Ultimately, a resilient mindset empowers individuals and communities to face challenges head-on, adapt to change, and emerge stronger than before.

The Strength of a Resilient Community

The strength of a resilient community lies in its ability to adapt, to support one another, and to thrive in the face of adversity. Resilient communities are not defined by their absence of challenges but by how they respond to those challenges. A community's strength comes from its collective ability to weather crises, learn from experiences, and work together toward recovery and growth. This resilience is built through strong connections, shared values, proactive planning, and a deep sense of responsibility to each other. Resilient communities foster a culture where individuals support one another, resources are pooled effectively, and solutions to problems are found collaboratively.

One of the key factors that contribute to the resilience of a community is its social fabric. A tight-knit community with strong relationships and networks is better equipped to handle adversity because people can rely on one another for emotional support, practical help, and problem-solving. For example, in the aftermath of a natural disaster like a flood or hurricane, resilient communities often rely on neighbors to assist with evacuation, provide temporary shelter, or help with rebuilding efforts. During the recovery period, individuals who share a sense of belonging and responsibility for each other are more likely to come together to address the collective needs of the community. In contrast, communities with weaker social ties may struggle to mobilize resources and may experience a longer and more painful recovery process.

Resilience in communities is also fostered through effective leadership and proactive planning. Leaders in resilient communities are not only responsive during crises but also anticipate potential challenges and work to create systems that can withstand adversity. For example, a community that invests in disaster preparedness plans—such as emergency response systems, evacuation routes, or communication networks—is better able to respond quickly and efficiently when a crisis strikes. In cities that face the threat of wildfires or hurricanes, local governments often engage in preparedness campaigns to ensure that residents know how to protect themselves and their homes. These efforts help communities stay calm and organized during disasters, reducing panic and ensuring a quicker recovery. Leaders also play a crucial role in fostering a culture of resilience by encouraging collaboration, resource-sharing, and long-term thinking.

Furthermore, economic resilience plays a significant role in a community's overall strength. Communities that have diversified economies, with a mix of industries, are better able to withstand financial shocks, such as economic recessions or sudden job losses. For instance, cities with strong local businesses, varied industries, and robust support networks can weather economic downturns more effectively than communities that rely heavily on one sector. A resilient community might support its local economy by shopping at small businesses, investing in community-driven projects, or creating programs that help workers transition to new industries when necessary. Additionally, communities that encourage entrepreneurship and innovation are better positioned to rebound after an economic setback. By creating a culture that values adaptability and new ideas, communities can navigate difficult times while continuing to grow.

Environmental resilience is also a key element in the strength of a community. Communities that take steps to protect their environment and build sustainable practices are better equipped to handle environmental challenges, such as natural disasters, climate change, and resource depletion. For example, communities that implement flood-prevention measures, such as green infrastructure or flood barriers, reduce the impact of heavy rains and rising water levels. Similarly, communities that focus on sustainable agriculture and energy use can mitigate the effects of climate change and create a more secure future for their residents. In the face of global challenges such as rising sea levels and extreme weather events, environmentally resilient communities are more adaptable, ensuring long-term sustainability and safety for future generations.

Education is another pillar of resilience. Communities that invest in education—both for young people and adults—are better prepared to face the future. Education empowers individuals with the knowledge and skills needed to adapt to new circumstances, solve problems, and contribute to the community's well-being. For example, communities with strong educational systems can equip their residents with the tools to rebuild after an economic downturn or natural disaster. Additionally, educational initiatives focused on climate change awareness, health, and sustainability can help future generations make informed decisions and take action to protect their communities. When communities emphasize lifelong learning and skill-building, they.

In conclusion, the strength of a resilient community is built on a foundation of strong social ties, proactive leadership, economic diversification, environmental sustainability, and a focus on health, education, and inclusivity. Resilient communities are not only able to survive challenges but can thrive and emerge stronger. Through collective effort, preparation, and a shared sense of responsibility, communities can face adversities with confidence, adapt to new circumstances, and continue to grow. By cultivating resilience in all aspects of life, communities can ensure that they are prepared for whatever the future holds and are empowered to overcome the challenges they face together.

CHAPTER 8

Leveraging Collective Strengths for Social Change

Leveraging collective strengths for social change is a powerful strategy for addressing complex societal challenges. When individuals and groups come together, pooling their knowledge, resources, and talents, they can create lasting change in ways that are often impossible to achieve alone. Collective action allows for a greater reach, a broader impact, and a stronger voice, especially when it comes to advocating for social justice, environmental sustainability, or community development. It transforms isolated efforts into coordinated movements that inspire change, challenge systemic issues, and promote equality. By harnessing the strengths of diverse groups, society can tackle the root causes of injustice and inequality, creating a more inclusive and equitable world.

One of the clearest examples of leveraging collective strengths for social change can be seen in the civil rights movements throughout history. In the United States, the efforts of activists, organizers, and everyday citizens working together through protests, legal challenges, and grassroots advocacy were instrumental in challenging racial segregation and discrimination. For instance, the Montgomery Bus Boycott of 1955–1956, which was sparked by the arrest of Rosa Parks, demonstrated the power of collective action. African American communities, alongside allies, united to boycott the city's buses, which eventually led to a Supreme Court ruling that declared bus segregation unconstitutional. This collective mobilization showed how when a community joins forces to challenge systemic inequality, they can achieve monumental shifts in societal norms and policies.

Another example of collective strength driving social change is seen in the global climate justice movement. Climate change is a complex issue that requires collaborative efforts from governments, corporations, activists, and individuals. Groups like Fridays for Future, led by young activists, have mobilized millions around the world to demand urgent action to combat climate change. Through protests, petitions, and partnerships with environmental organizations, they have raised global awareness and pushed leaders to commit to stronger environmental policies. This movement has shown how youth activism and collective advocacy can push for policy changes at the international level, highlighting how individual actions, when combined, can lead to collective power and spark social change on a global scale.

In the field of gender equality, collective strength has also played a crucial role in challenging and changing societal norms. The #MeToo movement, which began as a grassroots effort to raise awareness about sexual harassment and assault, grew into a worldwide movement, uniting women (and men) across the globe in a call for justice and systemic change. By sharing their personal stories and amplifying the voices of those who had been silenced for too long, the movement successfully brought issues of sexual violence and harassment to the forefront of public discourse. The collective strength of people coming together to support one another, share their experiences, and demand change has led to significant legal reforms, workplace policies, and shifts in cultural attitudes toward gender and power dynamics.

Community-driven change also exemplifies the power of collective strengths. In neighborhoods where resources are limited, residents often come together to improve their surroundings through initiatives such as community gardens, local food banks, and youth mentorship programs. For instance, in cities grappling with food insecurity, grassroots organizations have worked together to establish urban farms that provide fresh produce to underserved communities. These local efforts can help communities become more self-sufficient and resilient, improving access to food and promoting health and wellness. In these cases, leveraging collective strengths—whether through volunteer work, shared knowledge, or pooling resources—can have a significant impact on improving living conditions and addressing social inequalities.

In conclusion, leveraging collective strengths for social change is one of the most effective ways to create lasting, meaningful progress. Whether through grassroots movements, youth activism, or global collaborations, when people come together, they can address issues too vast and complex for any single individual or group to tackle alone. By pooling resources, sharing knowledge, and working collaboratively, society can create transformative change, tackling social injustices and improving lives on a large scale. Ultimately, collective action is about recognizing that each individual's contribution, when united with others, can create the collective power necessary to bring about social transformation and a more just and equitable world.

The Power of Collective Action

The power of collective action is one of the most profound forces for change in society. When individuals unite around a common cause, pooling their resources, skills, and energy, they can achieve far-reaching impacts that would be impossible for any single person or small group to accomplish alone. Collective action draws strength from collaboration, shared purpose, and mutual support, making it an essential driver for social, environmental, and political change. Throughout history and in contemporary movements, the effectiveness of collective action can be seen in its ability to challenge entrenched systems, influence policy, and inspire global movements for justice and equity.

One of the most notable examples of the power of collective action is the Civil Rights Movement in the United States during the 1950s and 1960s. The movement was fueled by the collective efforts of countless individuals and organizations, all working together to dismantle the systemic racism and segregation that had oppressed African Americans for centuries. Through protests, legal challenges, and grassroots organizing, the movement secured landmark legislative victories, including the Civil Rights Act of 1964 and the Voting Rights Act of 1965. What made these successes possible was the power of collective action—thousands of people coming together to demand change. From mass protests to sit-ins, from boycotts to the work of legal advocates, every form of collective effort contributed to the transformation of American society. This movement showed that when people from different walks of life unite with a common purpose, they can challenge deeply entrenched systems of oppression and achieve meaningful progress.

Environmental movements also demonstrate the power of collective action, particularly in the fight against climate change. One notable example is the global youth-led movement initiated by young activists around the world, including the Fridays for Future movement. Sparked by the efforts of a single activist in Sweden, this global campaign has grown into a worldwide call to action for addressing the climate crisis. Millions of students have participated in climate strikes, demanding that governments take immediate and bold action to combat climate change. The collective efforts of these young people, alongside scientists, environmental organizations, and concerned citizens, have raised global awareness and put pressure on political leaders to enact policies that protect the environment. The movement has led to increased climate commitments by governments, corporations, and international organizations. By amplifying the voices of youth and environmental advocates, collective action has sparked a worldwide conversation about climate change, resulting in policy shifts and greater recognition of the urgency of environmental issues.

Similarly, collective action is a driving force in efforts to protect human rights across the globe. One powerful example of this is the global campaign to end apartheid in South Africa. While the fight for equality in South Africa began within the country, it gained significant momentum due to the collective actions of international communities. People around the world engaged in boycotts, protests, and advocacy campaigns that pressured governments and corporations to stop supporting the apartheid regime. The international sanctions imposed on South Africa, coupled with the efforts of anti-apartheid activists, played a crucial role in dismantling the racist system of apartheid. This global solidarity effort demonstrated how collective action, across borders and cultures, can create pressure that forces governments to change policies and uphold human rights.

In the field of public health, collective action has been essential in addressing global health crises, such as the fight against the HIV/AIDS (human immunodeficiency virus/acquired immunodeficiency syndrome) epidemic. During the 1980s and 1990s, the HIV/AIDS crisis disproportionately affected marginalized communities, especially in sub-Saharan Africa. However, a coalition of governments, global health organizations, advocacy groups, and individuals worked together to raise awareness, promote education, and push for the development and distribution of lifesaving treatments. Through collective action, significant progress was made in combating the disease, reducing its stigma, and improving access to health care. Initiatives such as the Global Fund to Fight AIDS, Tuberculosis, and Malaria, along with grassroots activism, helped shift global policies, providing support to millions of people affected by the disease.

In recent years, collective action has also played a significant role in the global refugee crisis. As millions of refugees flee conflict, persecution, and economic hardship, individuals, governments, and organizations have united to provide humanitarian aid, shelter, and support. Whether through donations, volunteering, or advocating for refugee rights, collective efforts have been critical in addressing the needs of displaced individuals. Local communities, nongovernmental organizations (NGOs), and international bodies have worked together to provide resources, create safe spaces, and push for policy changes to improve the lives of refugees. While challenges remain, the global response to the refugee crisis highlights how collective action can provide essential support and drive systemic change.

In conclusion, the power of collective action is transformative, enabling individuals and groups to challenge the status quo; overcome significant challenges; and drive social, political, and environmental change. Whether through historical movements like civil rights, labor rights, and anti-apartheid efforts, or contemporary campaigns addressing climate change, human rights, and public health, collective action demonstrates the power of unity in creating a better world. By coming together, pooling resources, sharing knowledge, and amplifying their voices, people can accomplish what would be impossible alone, making collective action a crucial force for social change.

Empowering Individuals to Contribute to Change

Empowering individuals to contribute to change is a vital strategy in fostering social transformation and addressing the complex issues facing communities and societies. When people feel empowered, they are more likely to take action, contribute to collective efforts, and drive change in their personal lives and beyond. Empowerment enables individuals to recognize their own potential, build confidence, and understand their ability to make a difference in the world. This can lead to significant shifts in community dynamics, societal norms, and even global movements. By providing the tools, support, and opportunities for people to act, societies can unleash a wave of creativity, innovation, and advocacy that drives meaningful change.

A powerful example of how empowering individuals leads to social change can be seen in the realm of education. Across the world, many initiatives aim to empower individuals, particularly girls and women, by providing them with access to education. One notable example is the global movement to ensure girls' education, which has been championed by various organizations and activists. In regions where girls traditionally face barriers to education, such as in parts of sub-Saharan Africa or South Asia, empowering girls with education leads to transformative change. For instance, in countries like Afghanistan and Nigeria, efforts by local groups, supported by international organizations, have worked to ensure girls attend school and receive an education. This empowerment not only improves the lives of these girls but also contributes to broader societal change. Educated girls are more likely to become leaders, advocate for social justice, and contribute to their communities' economic development. In many cases, they become role models, inspiring others to pursue education and advocate for their own rights.

Empowerment also plays a crucial role in the realm of public health. In recent years, there has been a growing movement to empower individuals to take control of their own health and well-being. This has been particularly evident in the fight against diseases such as HIV/AIDS, where community-based efforts have made a significant impact on awareness, prevention, and treatment. In many countries, individuals living with HIV have been empowered to speak openly about their experiences, reduce stigma, and advocate for better health care access. For example, in South Africa, local HIV/AIDS activists, often those living with the disease, have played a critical role in challenging the stigma surrounding HIV/AIDS, educating communities, and pushing for more accessible treatments. These efforts have resulted in increased awareness, expanded health care access, and improved outcomes for people living with HIV/AIDS. By empowering individuals to share their stories and demand better services, communities have been able to make significant strides in the fight against the virus.

Similarly, the power of empowerment can be seen in grassroots movements for racial and social justice. The Black Lives Matter movement is a prime example of individuals coming together to demand justice and equality. What started as a hashtag on social media evolved into a global movement that has empowered individuals—particularly young people and people of color—to speak out against systemic racism, police brutality, and social inequities. The movement has provided a platform for marginalized voices and has inspired countless individuals to take action in their communities. Whether through protests, petitions, or social media campaigns, Black Lives Matter has empowered people to contribute to the broader conversation about racial equality. The movement has led to tangible changes, including police reform measures, a broader public dialogue about race, and an increase in voter turnout in communities historically underrepresented in political processes. This example shows that when individuals are empowered to act, even through small-scale efforts, they can create ripple effects that lead to societal transformation.

In the realm of social entrepreneurship, empowering individuals to create businesses that address social issues has been transformative. Social entrepreneurs are individuals who use innovative business solutions to solve pressing social problems. For example, many social enterprises focus on addressing issues like poverty, hunger, and access to clean water. One such example is the work of social enterprises that provide affordable solar energy to rural communities. In areas where electricity access is limited, social entrepreneurs have empowered individuals by offering affordable solar-powered devices that improve the quality of life. These businesses not only help individuals gain access to much-needed resources, but they also create local jobs and economic opportunities. By empowering entrepreneurs to create businesses that have both social and economic impacts, these initiatives demonstrate how individual actions can contribute to larger systemic change.

Another powerful example is seen in the movement for gender equality. Women and men who have been empowered with the tools and resources to challenge gender norms and fight for equal rights have played a crucial role in transforming societal structures. For example, in many parts of the world, women have led efforts to combat gender-based violence, advocating for stronger legal protections, increased resources for survivors, and societal shifts in attitudes toward violence. In countries like India, the #MeToo movement has empowered individuals to come forward with their stories of sexual harassment and assault, challenging long-held cultural taboos and demanding justice. As individuals gain the confidence to speak out, they contribute to a larger societal shift toward greater respect for gender equality. Through such movements, empowering individuals to take action can dismantle long-standing gender biases and create more inclusive societies.

In conclusion, empowering individuals to contribute to change is essential for creating a more just, equitable, and sustainable world. By providing people with the tools, support, and opportunities to take action, they can drive positive change in their own lives and in their communities. Whether in the fight for education, environmental sustainability, public health, racial justice, or gender equality, empowered individuals can challenge existing systems and create lasting social transformation. By nurturing and amplifying the voices of individuals, we can build movements that address the pressing issues of our time and create a future where everyone has the opportunity to contribute to change.

Creating Systems of Support for Change

Creating systems of support for change is crucial to ensuring that individual efforts are sustainable and impactful over time. Change, especially when it involves addressing systemic issues such as inequality, climate change, or public health crises, requires more than just individual action. It needs a supportive infrastructure that facilitates collaboration, provides resources, and ensures that those working for change have the tools and networks they need to succeed. These systems of support can take many forms, from community organizations and government programs to corporate social responsibility (CSR) initiatives and digital platforms. By creating robust support structures, we can foster an environment in which change is not only possible but also lasting.

One example of creating a system of support for change can be found in the growing network of NGOs working on issues like poverty alleviation, education, and health care. These organizations often serve as vital support systems for individuals and communities seeking change. For example, in many developing countries, NGOs provide critical resources such as educational materials, medical supplies, and vocational training. In countries where access to government services is limited, these organizations step in to fill the gap, creating systems of support that help empower communities to take charge of their own development. One such example is the work done by NGOs in regions like sub-Saharan Africa, where organizations focused on clean water access, health care, and education have worked with local communities to improve quality of life. By providing the infrastructure and resources needed for sustainable change, these organizations help create a long-term support system for the individuals they serve, empowering them to become agents of change in their own communities.

In the corporate world, creating systems of support for change can also play a crucial role. Companies that prioritize CSR and environmental sustainability can build systems of support for broader societal change by using their influence, resources, and networks. For example, companies like Patagonia have created business models that prioritize ethical sourcing, environmental protection, and fair labor practices. These businesses not only contribute to social change through their practices but also use their platforms to support grassroots movements, amplify causes, and encourage consumers to take action. By integrating social responsibility into their business models, companies can create an ecosystem where change is supported at multiple levels—individual, organizational, and societal. In the case of Patagonia, the company's commitment to environmental activism and sustainability serves as a model for other businesses to create similar systems of support for change, demonstrating how the private sector can contribute to social and environmental movements.

Education systems also serve as key support structures for individuals seeking change. Schools and universities can empower students with the knowledge, skills, and tools to become agents of change in their communities. Many universities have developed specialized programs, such as social entrepreneurship courses, leadership development programs, and environmental sustainability initiatives, that provide students with the framework for addressing global challenges. One example is the University of Cape Town's involvement in programs designed to combat climate change through research and local activism. By equipping students with knowledge and real-world experience, these educational institutions create a support system that helps young people lead change both locally and globally. This educational foundation creates a network of change-makers who can collaborate with others in the field, share resources, and implement ideas effectively. The support provided by such programs nurtures an environment where innovation and progress are actively encouraged, fostering the next generation of leaders in social, political, and environmental change.

In the digital age, technology has also become a key component of support systems for change. Social media platforms, crowdfunding sites, and digital tools have created virtual ecosystems where individuals and organizations can share ideas, raise awareness, and gain financial and social support for their initiatives. For example, crowdfunding platforms like GoFundMe or Kickstarter allow individuals to raise funds for social projects, from medical expenses to community development initiatives. These platforms enable people from all over the world to support causes they believe in, creating a network of financial and emotional backing for those working to create change. Similarly, social media networks like Twitter, Instagram, and Facebook have become vital tools for organizing campaigns, spreading awareness, and rallying people together for collective action. The Arab Spring, which was driven in large part by social media, shows how digital tools can be part of a larger system of support that helps individuals organize and amplify their calls for change. By providing an accessible platform for voices to be heard, social media has empowered individuals to challenge oppressive regimes and advocate for democracy, showing how digital platforms can become powerful systems of support for social and political movements.

Finally, creating systems of support for change also involves fostering strong community networks. Community-based organizations and local groups are essential for providing the social infrastructure that supports individual and collective action. These groups can offer emotional support, build solidarity, and provide practical resources such as food, shelter, or childcare. In times of crisis, such as natural disasters or economic hardships, local communities often become the first line of support for those in need. For example, during the aftermath of Hurricane Katrina, community organizations in New Orleans played a critical role in providing shelter, food, and other forms of aid to survivors. These grassroots efforts not only address immediate needs but also build long-term resilience within communities. By creating a network of support at the local level, communities can foster social change from the ground up, empowering individuals to take charge of their own futures while contributing to larger societal shifts.

In conclusion, creating systems of support for change is fundamental to ensuring that efforts to address social, political, and environmental challenges are successful and sustainable. Whether through government policies, grassroots organizations, corporate responsibility initiatives, or digital platforms, these support structures provide the foundation for individuals to take meaningful action and drive collective change. By investing in and building these systems, societies can empower individuals to contribute to lasting transformations, creating a more equitable, sustainable, and just world.

Addressing Systemic Challenges

Addressing systemic challenges is crucial for creating lasting social, economic, and environmental change. Systemic challenges are deep-rooted problems that affect the very structure and functioning of societies, economies, or institutions. These challenges are not isolated incidents but are built into the systems themselves, often perpetuating cycles of inequality, injustice, and inefficiency. Tackling these issues requires a comprehensive approach that goes beyond short-term fixes and addresses the root causes, creating long-term solutions that benefit all members of society. Whether it's economic inequality, racial discrimination, climate change, or public health crises, addressing systemic challenges requires collective action, policy reform, and a commitment to dismantling the structures that perpetuate these problems.

One of the most pressing systemic challenges is economic inequality, which affects millions of people worldwide. Economic inequality is often the result of structural factors such as unequal access to education, health care, and employment opportunities. In many countries, wealth is concentrated in the hands of a small percentage of the population, while large segments of the population struggle to meet basic needs. Efforts to address economic inequality, such as movements advocating for a living wage, aim to challenge the systemic wage disparities that exist between low-income workers and those in higher-paying jobs. Through collective action, lobbying, and grassroots organizing, these movements seek to bring about changes in wage policies and improve the living standards of disadvantaged groups. The changes achieved through these efforts show how addressing systemic inequality can lead to a more just and equitable society. While challenges remain, these movements highlight the importance of addressing the root causes of economic inequality to create long-term social change.

Racial discrimination is another example of a systemic challenge that requires concerted efforts to address. In many countries, deeply entrenched systems of racial inequality continue to affect access to education, employment, housing, and justice. The criminal justice system, in particular, often disproportionately affects racial minorities, with individuals of the latter facing higher rates of arrest, incarceration, and harsher sentencing. Movements advocating for changes in policing practices, sentencing laws, and prison reform work to dismantle the structures that perpetuate racial injustice. These movements call for legal reforms and public policy changes aimed at reducing racial disparities. Additionally, efforts to reform educational systems, health care access, and employment opportunities are essential to ensure equal access and fair treatment for all people, regardless of race. By confronting the root causes of racial discrimination, societies can begin to dismantle institutional barriers and create a more inclusive and equitable environment for all individuals.

Climate change is a global, systemic challenge that requires immediate and coordinated action. The environmental crisis, driven by carbon emissions, deforestation, and industrial pollution, affects ecosystems, weather patterns, and the livelihoods of millions of people. Climate change is not just an environmental issue but also a social and economic one, as vulnerable communities often bear the brunt of its impact. Addressing the systemic drivers of environmental destruction, such as unsustainable industrial practices and reliance on fossil fuels, is critical for mitigating climate change. Global initiatives focused on limiting global warming, adopting renewable energy sources, and promoting sustainable practices are steps toward addressing the systemic causes of climate change. To fully tackle the crisis, broader systemic shifts in consumption patterns, energy production, and infrastructure must take place. This requires collaboration among governments, businesses, and individuals to move toward more sustainable practices and reduce the environmental footprint of industries.

Education is another area where systemic challenges are prevalent, especially in underserved communities. In many parts of the world, children from low-income families face barriers to accessing quality education, such as a lack of proper facilities, trained teachers, or basic learning materials. Public education systems often reflect economic and racial divides, with schools in wealthier neighborhoods receiving better funding and resources compared to those in poorer areas. To address these systemic challenges, reforms must focus on equitable funding for schools, increased access to quality teaching, and community involvement in educational decision making. Programs designed to reduce the achievement gap by providing financial assistance, mentorship, and after-school programs can help ensure that every student, regardless of their background, has an equal opportunity to succeed.

Systemic challenges also extend to gender inequality, which continues to affect women and girls around the world. Gender-based violence, pay inequality, and underrepresentation in leadership roles are just a few examples of systemic barriers that women face. In many societies, laws and cultural norms continue to discriminate against women, limiting their opportunities for education, employment, and participation in decision-making processes. Addressing gender inequality requires legal reforms to ensure equal rights for women in the workplace, in politics, and in education. Public campaigns aimed at changing societal attitudes toward gender roles and violence are also essential in challenging the deep-seated biases that perpetuate discrimination. Moreover, increasing female representation in leadership positions across various sectors is necessary to ensure that women's voices are heard and that gender equality is prioritized in policy making and decision making. By addressing these systemic issues, we can create more inclusive societies where gender equality is the norm rather than the exception.

In conclusion, addressing systemic challenges requires a comprehensive, multifaceted approach that tackles the root causes of inequality, injustice, and inefficiency. Whether in economic systems, criminal justice, health care, education, or environmental sustainability, systemic problems can only be solved by dismantling the structures that perpetuate them. By advocating for policy reforms, empowering marginalized communities, and fostering collaboration at all levels of society, we can create the conditions for meaningful and lasting change. Only by addressing these systemic issues head-on can we build a more just, equitable, and sustainable world for future generations.

Social Change Through Collective Growth

Social change through collective growth is a powerful and transformative process that occurs when individuals, communities, and organizations come together to address systemic issues, foster collaboration, and work toward a common goal. This type of change is driven by the collective efforts of many individuals who share a vision for a more just, equitable, and sustainable world. While individual actions are important, it is through collective growth that deep, lasting change is achieved. By leveraging the strengths of various groups and fostering a spirit of collaboration, societies can overcome long-standing challenges and create a future that benefits everyone.

One of the key drivers of social change through collective growth is the power of community organizing. When individuals unite around a common cause, they can amplify their voices and demand the changes that are needed. Grassroots movements, for example, have been instrumental in advocating for civil rights, environmental protection, and gender equality. These movements, often led by communities most affected by systemic inequalities, have had a lasting impact on public policies and societal attitudes. By organizing at the local level, individuals create networks of support, share resources, and build solidarity, which enables them to address challenges that might otherwise seem insurmountable. This collective action not only brings about changes in laws and policies but also shifts cultural norms and societal values, paving the way for long-term social transformation.

Collective growth is fueled by partnerships between different sectors, such as government, business, and civil society. When these sectors collaborate and align their efforts, they can create systemic change on a larger scale. For instance, businesses that prioritize CSR can work alongside NGOs and governments to address pressing social and environmental issues. These partnerships can result in significant investments in education, health care, clean energy, and community development. When businesses, governments, and civil society organizations work together to solve problems, they can pool resources, expertise, and influence, making it easier to implement sustainable solutions that benefit everyone. This type of collective growth ensures that efforts are coordinated and that the impact of social change is magnified.

Another example of collective growth leading to social change can be seen in the environmental movement. Environmental issues, such as climate change, deforestation, and pollution, are global challenges that require collective action. Local communities, environmental activists, scientists, governments, and businesses must work together to address these issues on a systemic level. By engaging communities in sustainable practices, advocating for policy changes, and raising awareness through media campaigns, collective action can bring about meaningful environmental reforms. As more individuals and organizations understand the importance of environmental conservation and adopt sustainable practices, collective growth accelerates the momentum toward global environmental change. This type of collaboration not only addresses immediate concerns but also creates a cultural shift toward more sustainable living.

Social change through collective growth also fosters the development of inclusive communities where diverse voices are heard and valued. By creating platforms that allow for the participation of marginalized groups, societies can build more equitable systems that address the needs of everyone, rather than just a select few. For example, movements focused on gender equality, racial justice, and disability rights often bring together people from diverse backgrounds and experiences to work toward common goals. The inclusion of different perspectives leads to more comprehensive solutions that are responsive to the unique challenges faced by various communities. This type of collective growth ensures that social change is inclusive and reflects the needs and desires of all members of society.

In conclusion, social change through collective growth is not only possible but essential for building a more just, equitable, and sustainable future. When individuals, communities, organizations, and governments come together to address systemic challenges, the impact of their collective efforts can be far-reaching. By empowering individuals through education, fostering collaboration across sectors, leveraging technology, and building inclusive communities, we can create lasting change that benefits all members of society. The process of collective growth ensures that no one is left behind and that social change is achieved through the combined efforts of many, making it a more powerful and transformative force for good.

CHAPTER 9

Measuring Impact and Sustaining Long-Term Growth

Measuring impact and sustaining long-term growth are integral to ensuring that initiatives—whether in the nonprofit, business, social, or environmental sectors—continue to create meaningful change over time. While immediate results may be encouraging, lasting growth requires ongoing evaluation and adaptation to maintain momentum and address emerging challenges. Without consistent impact measurement, it's difficult to determine if efforts are achieving their intended outcomes or if resources are being used effectively. Furthermore, long-term growth necessitates a commitment to continuous improvement, innovation, and scalability to expand the reach and effectiveness of programs or initiatives.

For example, in the realm of international development, organizations working to reduce poverty or improve access to education must not only measure the short-term success of their programs—such as the number of people reached or the immediate improvements in educational outcomes—but also track long-term outcomes. Are these individuals able to sustain the gains they've made? Do children who receive better schooling in the short term go on to graduate and secure stable employment? Are the communities themselves becoming more resilient over time, able to adapt and thrive without ongoing outside support? Measuring these long-term outcomes allows organizations to understand the true effectiveness of their programs and adjust their strategies accordingly. In some cases, it may reveal the need for additional interventions or highlight areas where sustainable change has yet to be achieved.

In the business sector, companies focused on corporate social responsibility (CSR) or sustainability must continually measure the impact of their initiatives on both their bottom line and broader societal outcomes. For instance, a company that has launched a program to reduce its carbon footprint can measure short-term results, such as a decrease in energy consumption or reductions in waste. However, to sustain long-term growth, it must also track long-term outcomes like shifts in consumer behavior, employee engagement, and brand loyalty. Long-term success in sustainability initiatives often hinges on changing industry practices, influencing supply chain partners, and creating innovations that drive systemic environmental benefits. The company must stay vigilant about evolving industry standards, maintain transparency in its environmental impact, and be adaptable to regulatory changes or shifts in public opinion. Through continuous monitoring and impact measurement, businesses can ensure that their sustainability efforts are not only achieving short-term gains but are also contributing to lasting positive change.

In social movements, measuring impact is crucial to understanding how efforts translate into long-term societal shifts. For example, movements for racial justice or gender equality often make significant strides in raising awareness and influencing public opinion in the short term. However, to sustain long-term growth and effect systemic change, these movements must track progress over time. Metrics might include the implementation of policies that close the wage gap, improvements in representation in leadership positions, reductions in discrimination, and shifts in cultural attitudes. Tracking these indicators over the long term ensures that progress is not only maintained but that efforts are recalibrated to address challenges as they arise. The sustained growth of a social movement is also tied to its ability to inspire and mobilize future generations, ensuring that the momentum is carried forward by those who will continue the fight for equality and justice.

Measuring impact over time also helps identify potential risks and challenges that could hinder long-term success. For example, in health care, a program designed to reduce child mortality rates might see initial success in improving access to medical care or vaccination coverage. However, over time, it's essential to track whether those improvements lead to sustained health outcomes, such as lower mortality rates, better nutrition, and improved maternal health. Programs must be flexible enough to address emerging health threats, such as new diseases or changing environmental conditions, and adjust strategies as needed. Long-term growth in health care initiatives requires a comprehensive understanding of both the immediate and long-term factors that influence health outcomes, as well as the ability to adapt to evolving challenges.

Ultimately, measuring impact and sustaining long-term growth are intertwined processes that require continuous evaluation, adaptability, and collaboration. Without effective impact measurement, it's impossible to know whether progress is being made or if strategies need to be adjusted to improve outcomes. At the same time, long-term growth cannot be achieved without understanding and addressing the factors that contribute to sustainable success. Organizations, businesses, governments, and communities must commit to ongoing measurement and analysis to ensure that their efforts not only produce immediate benefits but also create lasting, positive change. By prioritizing both impact measurement and sustainability, they can maximize the effectiveness of their initiatives, adapt to new challenges, and build a foundation for long-term progress.

The Importance of Measuring Impact

Measuring impact is a crucial component of any initiative aimed at creating social, environmental, or economic change. Without clear metrics and systems to evaluate progress, it becomes difficult to determine whether efforts are successful, identify areas for improvement, or justify continued investment in programs. Whether in the context of nonprofit organizations, social enterprises, community programs, or CSR initiatives, measuring impact allows stakeholders to understand how their actions are contributing to their goals and to make informed decisions based on evidence. Impact measurement provides transparency, accountability, and insights that are essential for the effectiveness and sustainability of initiatives.

In the business world, measuring impact is equally important, especially for companies involved in CSR or sustainability initiatives. Businesses are increasingly held accountable by consumers, investors, and governments for the environmental and social impacts of their operations. For example, a company that implements a sustainability program to reduce its carbon footprint might track its progress by measuring reductions in greenhouse gas emissions, energy consumption, or waste generation. Similarly, companies might measure the impact of their philanthropic efforts, such as donations to charitable causes or partnerships with local communities. By measuring these impacts, businesses can demonstrate their commitment to sustainability, enhance their brand reputation, and attract socially conscious consumers and investors. Furthermore, measuring impact helps businesses understand which practices are most effective and where improvements can be made to ensure that their efforts align with long-term goals.

In the context of environmental initiatives, measuring impact is essential for understanding the effectiveness of conservation and sustainability efforts. For example, in projects aimed at reducing deforestation, impact might be measured by tracking changes in forest cover, biodiversity, and the health of local ecosystems. A project that promotes sustainable agriculture might measure the long-term impact on soil health, water usage, and local food security. Similarly, in wildlife conservation efforts, the success of reintroduction programs can be assessed by monitoring animal populations, genetic diversity, and habitat quality. By collecting and analyzing data on these indicators, organizations and governments can determine whether their conservation efforts are achieving their desired outcomes and make adjustments as needed. Additionally, measuring impact allows stakeholders to communicate progress to the public and to secure funding or support for future initiatives.

In education, measuring impact plays a critical role in determining whether interventions are effectively improving student outcomes. For example, if a program is introduced to help struggling students improve their math skills, its impact can be measured by assessing changes in test scores, teacher evaluations, and student engagement. Beyond academic achievement, measuring impact can also involve looking at broader outcomes, such as students' emotional well-being, social skills, or long-term educational attainment. In the case of online learning platforms or ed-tech initiatives, measuring impact might include tracking student retention rates, learning outcomes, and user feedback to assess the quality and accessibility of the platform. By measuring these different aspects of impact, educators and program administrators can continuously improve their strategies and ensure that students are receiving the support they need to succeed.

Public health initiatives also rely on impact measurement to assess their effectiveness and guide future interventions. For instance, a public health campaign aimed at increasing vaccination rates might measure success by tracking vaccination coverage, disease incidence, and public awareness levels. Similarly, programs designed to reduce smoking or promote healthy eating may measure impact by monitoring changes in behavior, health care costs, or the incidence of related diseases. Impact measurement in public health is crucial for understanding whether programs are reaching the right populations, whether the interventions are effective in changing health behaviors, and whether the desired health outcomes are being achieved. This data can inform policy decisions, help allocate resources more effectively, and shape future public health interventions.

Measuring impact is not only essential for evaluating the success of individual programs or projects but also for assessing larger systemic changes. For instance, social movements advocating for gender equality or racial justice may measure impact by tracking changes in public opinion, policy changes, representation in leadership positions, or disparities in income and opportunity. These movements often require long-term efforts, and measuring impact over time allows advocates to assess progress and adjust their strategies as needed. The measurement of impact in these cases may include qualitative data, such as personal stories or testimonies, as well as quantitative data that reflects changes in society. These efforts demonstrate that impact measurement can be both broad and nuanced, encompassing both measurable outcomes and more subjective shifts in attitudes and behavior.

Moreover, impact measurement helps identify areas where improvements are necessary. For example, in a community development project, initial goals may have been met, but data could reveal gaps in services or unmet needs within certain groups. By continuously evaluating impact, program leaders can identify these gaps, reallocate resources, and refine their strategies to better serve the community. This ongoing evaluation process ensures that initiatives remain responsive to the evolving needs of their target populations, ultimately leading to more effective and sustainable outcomes.

In conclusion, measuring impact is essential for ensuring the success and sustainability of any initiative aimed at creating social, environmental, or economic change. Whether in nonprofit work, business, public health, or education, tracking progress and evaluating outcomes allows stakeholders to assess the effectiveness of their efforts, make data-driven decisions, and communicate their successes to a wider audience. It enables organizations to continuously improve their strategies, align efforts with their goals, and demonstrate accountability to funders, partners, and the communities they serve. Ultimately, measuring impact provides the foundation for scaling successful programs and achieving long-term change.

Quantitative Methods of Measurement

Quantitative methods of measurement are essential tools used to assess and evaluate various aspects of a program, initiative, or project. These methods involve the collection and analysis of numerical data to provide objective insights into performance, progress, and outcomes. By focusing on measurable and quantifiable factors, quantitative methods allow for a more systematic and standardized way of evaluating impact. These methods are particularly valuable because they provide concrete data that can be analyzed to identify trends, measure effectiveness, and inform decision making.

One of the most common quantitative methods is surveys and questionnaires, which collect numerical data from respondents about their experiences, opinions, or behaviors. For example, a nonprofit organization that offers job training services might use a pre- and post-training survey to assess the effectiveness of its program. The survey could ask participants to rate their skills before and after the training on a scale from 1 to 10, with the results providing measurable data on how much improvement occurred. In this case, the quantitative data gathered can be used to determine the extent to which the training program has helped participants enhance their skills, and whether the results justify the investment in the program.

In the business world, key performance indicators (KPIs) are frequently used as quantitative measures to assess business performance and impact. KPIs can encompass a wide range of factors depending on the objectives of the business, such as sales figures, customer satisfaction scores, or website traffic. For instance, a company focused on improving its customer service might use customer satisfaction surveys to collect numerical ratings (e.g., a scale of 1–5) and calculate the average score. These quantitative measures provide clear insights into customer satisfaction and allow businesses to track their performance over time. If the KPI score improves, the business knows its customer service initiatives are working; if it declines, corrective action can be taken.

In education, test scores are often used as a quantitative method to measure the effectiveness of teaching strategies or student performance. For example, standardized tests, such as national exams, can be used to assess students' knowledge in subjects like mathematics, science, or reading. Educators can analyze test scores to gauge the success of a particular curriculum or teaching method. If students' test scores improve over time, it can be inferred that the teaching strategies employed are effective in enhancing student learning. Conversely, if scores remain stagnant or decline, it suggests that adjustments to the curriculum or instructional methods are needed.

Financial metrics also provide valuable quantitative measures in many industries. In the context of nonprofits, for example, measuring the cost per outcome is a useful way to assess the efficiency and effectiveness of a program. If a nonprofit organization is providing clean drinking water to rural communities, it can calculate the cost per person served to determine whether the program is achieving its goals efficiently. By tracking financial metrics like return on investment (ROI), nonprofits can measure the cost-effectiveness of their interventions and identify areas where resources might be better allocated to achieve greater impact.

In the field of environmental conservation, environmental indicators such as carbon emissions, water usage, or deforestation rates provide quantitative measures of progress. For instance, a program aimed at reducing carbon emissions might track metrics like the number of tons of CO_2 reduced over time. These data points help to evaluate the success of the program and demonstrate its impact in a way that is both measurable and tangible. By comparing these metrics to baseline data, organizations can determine whether they are on track to meet their sustainability goals. Similarly, tracking deforestation rates in a specific region can help conservationists measure the effectiveness of their reforestation efforts. The quantitative data provides concrete evidence of whether environmental preservation efforts are succeeding.

Benchmarking is another useful quantitative method that involves comparing a program's performance against established standards or the performance of similar organizations or initiatives. For instance, a company looking to improve employee productivity might compare its current output per employee with industry standards or with the performance of its competitors. This comparison allows businesses to gauge how well they are performing and identify areas for improvement. Benchmarking can also be applied to social programs, such as comparing the graduation rates of schools in different districts or assessing the poverty reduction efforts of various regions. Through benchmarking, organizations can learn from others and adopt best practices to enhance their own performance.

Lastly, data visualization is a powerful tool for presenting quantitative data in a way that is easy to interpret and understand. Using charts, graphs, and dashboards, data visualization allows stakeholders to quickly grasp trends, patterns, and relationships within the data. For example, a government agency might use data visualization to display the progress of a vaccination campaign, showing the number of people vaccinated over time across different regions. These visualizations help to highlight areas where the campaign is succeeding and identify regions that may require additional resources or outreach. By presenting data in a clear and accessible format, data visualization enhances decision making and makes it easier to communicate results to a broader audience.

In conclusion, quantitative methods of measurement provide valuable insights into the effectiveness of various programs and initiatives by focusing on measurable data and outcomes. Whether through surveys, statistical analysis, test scores, financial metrics, or environmental indicators, these methods allow organizations to track their progress, make informed decisions, and demonstrate their impact. By using quantitative methods, organizations can assess their performance, identify areas for improvement, and ultimately work toward achieving their goals in a more efficient and effective manner.

Qualitative Methods of Measurement

Qualitative methods of measurement focus on capturing the underlying qualities, experiences, and perspectives that contribute to a deeper understanding of a program or initiative's impact. Unlike quantitative methods, which rely on numerical data, qualitative methods prioritize narrative, subjective, and descriptive information. These methods are particularly valuable when it comes to understanding the complexities of human behavior, motivations, and experiences that numbers alone cannot fully explain. They allow researchers and organizations to explore the richness of a situation, provide insights into how and why changes occur, and offer a more holistic understanding of outcomes.

One common qualitative method is interviews, where individuals are asked open-ended questions to explore their views, experiences, and attitudes. For example, in a community development program focused on improving access to health care, program leaders might conduct interviews with residents to understand how health care services have impacted their lives. The interviews could explore areas such as personal health improvements, changes in health-seeking behavior, or challenges faced in accessing care. The insights gained from these interviews help to capture the human side of the program's impact, revealing factors that could influence the program's success or areas where it might be improved.

Observations are also widely used as a qualitative method, where researchers or program evaluators observe participants in their natural environment to understand behaviors, interactions, and dynamics. For example, in a workplace program aimed at improving teamwork and collaboration, an evaluator might observe how employees interact during team meetings or group activities. Through these observations, the evaluator can gain insights into team dynamics, communication patterns, and the effectiveness of collaboration strategies. Observational methods are particularly useful for capturing nonverbal cues, interpersonal relationships, and contextual factors that quantitative data might overlook.

Content analysis is another important qualitative method, where researchers analyze texts, media, or other forms of communication to identify patterns, themes, or insights. For instance, an organization may analyze social media posts or news articles related to a public health campaign to understand public perceptions and attitudes. By categorizing and interpreting these communications, content analysis can provide insights into how messages are being received by different audiences, identify gaps in understanding, and guide future messaging. In this way, content analysis can help determine the effectiveness of communication strategies and whether the intended messages are resonating with the target audience.

In narrative analysis, researchers examine stories or personal accounts to understand the meaning people attach to their experiences. This method is particularly useful in fields like psychology, education, and health care, where individuals' personal stories provide rich insights into their lived experiences. For example, a health organization might collect personal stories from cancer survivors to understand their journey through diagnosis, treatment, and recovery. By analyzing these narratives, the organization can uncover key factors that contribute to the survivor's resilience, coping strategies, and overall well-being. Narrative analysis helps organizations gain a deeper understanding of how individuals make sense of their experiences and how these experiences shape their perspectives on health or other topics.

Ethnography is a more immersive qualitative method that involves researchers becoming involved in the community or setting they are studying. In an ethnographic study, the researcher might live or work alongside participants, engaging directly with them to gather a comprehensive understanding of their behaviors, values, and social dynamics. For example, an ethnographer studying a rural agricultural community might spend several months working with local farmers, attending community meetings, and participating in daily activities. This approach provides an insider's perspective on the cultural and social contexts that influence people's actions, decisions, and outcomes. Ethnography is a powerful method for capturing the complexities of a community or group, particularly when trying to understand deeply ingrained social norms or long-standing issues.

Finally, the Delphi method involves gathering insights from a group of experts through a series of rounds of questioning. In each round, participants provide their opinions or predictions on a particular topic, and their responses are compiled and shared with the group. Experts are then asked to reconsider their responses in light of others' input, which helps to refine and clarify the collective insights. This method is often used in fields like public policy or technology forecasting, where expert opinions are essential to understanding complex, evolving issues. The Delphi method allows for the accumulation of expert knowledge and helps build a consensus on important decisions or predictions.

In conclusion, qualitative methods of measurement provide in-depth insights into the human experiences, perceptions, and social contexts that quantitative data might miss. Through interviews, focus groups, case studies, observations, and other approaches, qualitative research captures the nuances and complexities of a situation, offering valuable perspectives on program effectiveness, individual experiences, and organizational challenges. By using qualitative methods, organizations can gain a more comprehensive understanding of their impact, improve decision making, and develop more responsive and adaptive strategies for future success.

Feedback Loops: The Key to Continuous Improvement

Feedback loops are essential mechanisms that allow individuals, teams, and organizations to continuously improve their processes, products, and performance. A feedback loop involves gathering feedback, analyzing it, and using that information to make adjustments or changes that lead to better outcomes. The concept of a feedback loop is applicable in many areas, from business to education to personal development, and plays a critical role in fostering growth and adaptability.

One example of feedback loops in action is in the context of customer service. Many businesses regularly solicit feedback from customers through surveys or follow-up emails. When a customer has a negative experience, the feedback collected helps the company identify the root causes of dissatisfaction, such as slow service or poor product quality. The company can then use this information to make improvements, such as training staff to provide better service, implementing faster service procedures, or improving product quality. As the business continues to gather feedback over time, it can track whether these changes have led to higher customer satisfaction, creating a continuous loop of assessment and improvement.

In education, feedback loops are vital for both student and teacher growth. For example, a teacher might assign a project and provide detailed feedback on students' work. When students receive feedback, they can use it to improve their next assignment or approach. Similarly, teachers can receive feedback from students about how effective their teaching methods are, allowing them to adjust their approach to suit students' learning styles. For instance, if students indicate that they struggle to understand a particular concept, the teacher may decide to adjust their lesson plans, offer additional resources, or use different teaching techniques. Over time, this iterative process creates a loop that helps improve both teaching and learning experiences.

Another example of feedback loops can be found in product development, where companies use customer feedback to refine their products. In the technology industry, for instance, software developers often release a beta version of a product and collect user feedback on functionality, user experience, and bugs. Based on this input, the developers make adjustments before the full product is launched. This feedback loop allows the product to evolve with customer needs and preferences, ensuring that the final product is well-received. Even after the launch, companies often continue to collect user feedback to refine the product further, creating an ongoing cycle of improvement.

In health care, feedback loops are used to ensure that patient care is continuously improving. For example, medical professionals might ask patients to rate their experiences or provide feedback on the quality of care they received. If patients report delays, inadequate explanations, or other concerns, health care providers can use this feedback to address specific issues. Over time, hospitals and clinics implement changes based on this feedback, such as improving wait times, enhancing communication between staff and patients, or adjusting treatment protocols. As these changes are made, patient satisfaction improves, and more feedback is gathered, reinforcing a loop that drives better care.

Feedback loops also play a crucial role in personal development. For individuals working to improve their skills or achieve personal goals, self-reflection is a key part of the feedback loop. For example, someone learning a new language might practice speaking and then ask a teacher or a peer for feedback on their pronunciation or grammar. They can then apply this feedback by making corrections and practicing again. Over time, with consistent feedback and application, their language skills improve. Similarly, someone working on fitness goals may track their progress and adjust their workout routine based on feedback from their body or a fitness coach, improving over time.

In the environmental sector, feedback loops are integral to sustainability initiatives. For example, a community working to reduce waste might track the volume of waste produced each month and ask residents for feedback on the effectiveness of recycling programs. If the community finds that recycling rates are low, they might take actions like educating residents, providing more recycling bins, or implementing incentive programs. By continuously collecting feedback and making improvements based on this input, the community can move toward its environmental goals in a way that is both sustainable and effective.

Feedback loops also play a significant role in policy making and governance. Governments and organizations often gather public input through surveys, town hall meetings, and consultations to understand the needs and opinions of citizens. For example, a local government might introduce a new public transportation initiative and gather feedback from commuters on service quality, affordability, and accessibility. The insights from the public can then guide adjustments to the program, such as changing routes, adjusting schedules, or improving accessibility. This feedback process ensures that policies are responsive to the needs of the community and can be improved based on real-world data.

In conclusion, feedback loops are powerful tools that drive continuous improvement across various sectors. Whether in business, education, health care, personal development, or environmental sustainability, feedback loops create an ongoing process of evaluation, adjustment, and refinement. By actively seeking and applying feedback, organizations and individuals can evolve, adapt, and grow. The consistent cycle of assessing, learning, and improving leads to better outcomes, increased efficiency, and sustained growth over time.

Sustaining Long-Term Growth

Sustaining long-term growth is a critical goal for individuals, organizations, and communities. It requires a strategic approach that not only focuses on short-term success but also builds resilience, fosters continuous improvement, and adapts to changing conditions over time. Long-term growth is driven by a combination of forward-thinking, resource management, and the ability to navigate challenges effectively. It also involves aligning goals with values and ensuring that growth is sustainable and inclusive.

One key factor in sustaining long-term growth is maintaining a strong foundation of trust and collaboration. For businesses, long-term success depends on building relationships with customers, employees, suppliers, and other stakeholders. For example, companies that prioritize customer satisfaction and continually seek feedback are more likely to build lasting loyalty. A business that values its employees by offering career development opportunities, providing a supportive work environment, and encouraging open communication is also more likely to retain talent and foster a culture of growth. This ongoing investment in people and relationships creates a stable foundation that supports long-term growth.

In the context of entrepreneurship, sustaining long-term growth involves being adaptable and resilient to market changes. For instance, a tech startup may begin by developing one product but will need to diversify its offerings over time to stay relevant as technology evolves. The company may invest in research and development, explore new markets, or innovate within its existing product lines to maintain its growth trajectory. An example of this can be seen in companies that started with one core product but expanded their range as consumer demands changed. For example, businesses that initially focused on a single service may expand into new areas, allowing them to tap into new customer bases and mitigate risks associated with market saturation. These businesses remain agile, adjusting their strategy in response to emerging trends and challenges.

Another aspect of sustaining long-term growth is the ability to develop and maintain systems of support. This can be particularly important for nonprofits or social enterprises that are focused on creating lasting social change. For example, a nonprofit organization focused on providing education in underserved communities might partner with other organizations, government agencies, or private sector companies to enhance its impact. These partnerships create a network of resources, knowledge, and expertise that support the organization's long-term mission. Through collaboration, nonprofits can leverage the collective strengths of others to overcome obstacles and scale their impact over time.

In education, long-term growth can be sustained by continuously evolving teaching methods and embracing technological advancements.

Schools that invest in professional development for teachers and encourage innovation in the classroom are better equipped to adapt to changes in student needs, curriculum requirements, and educational technology. An example of this is seen in schools that incorporate digital learning tools and interactive platforms into their teaching. By embracing these technologies, educators can better engage students, meet diverse learning styles, and prepare them for a rapidly changing world. Schools that continually invest in new resources and teaching strategies create a culture of growth and ensure that students remain prepared for future success.

In the public sector, sustaining long-term growth often requires a commitment to policy innovation and careful resource management. Governments that prioritize long-term infrastructure development, such as improving transportation networks or investing in renewable energy, ensure that their communities are prepared for future growth. For instance, cities that invest in green infrastructure—such as parks, sustainable buildings, and energy-efficient systems—are better positioned to thrive in the long run. These investments create more livable, resilient communities that can withstand economic and environmental changes, ultimately supporting long-term growth.

Sustaining long-term growth also requires an ability to measure progress and make adjustments as needed. Without regular evaluation, it is difficult to know whether the strategies in place are working or whether adjustments are needed. For businesses, this could mean tracking KPIs such as revenue growth, customer retention, and employee satisfaction. Regularly assessing these metrics allows organizations to make data-driven decisions that support continued growth. For individuals, this could involve periodically revisiting personal or professional goals to see if they are still aligned with their evolving aspirations. Regular reflection and assessment enable course corrections and ensure that long-term growth is both achievable and sustainable.

In agriculture, sustaining long-term growth involves adopting sustainable farming practices that protect the environment while ensuring economic viability. Farmers who adopt practices like crop rotation, reduced pesticide use, and water conservation techniques are able to maintain healthy soil and ecosystems, which support long-term agricultural productivity. These sustainable practices help ensure that farming remains

profitable and viable for future generations, rather than depleting resources in the short term. For example, organic farming techniques that
focus on environmental health and biodiversity can create more resilient
and sustainable food systems.

Finally, sustaining long-term growth involves resilience in the face of
setbacks and challenges. Economic downturns, natural disasters, or un-
foreseen global events—such as the COVID-19 pandemic—can test the
strength of organizations and communities. However, those that have built
a strong foundation of trust, collaboration, and adaptability are more likely
to weather such storms. For example, businesses that rapidly shifted to re-
mote work and invested in digital tools during the pandemic were able to
continue operations, protect their employees, and maintain growth, even
during a time of crisis. The ability to bounce back from adversity and continue forward is a critical factor in sustaining long-term growth.

In conclusion, sustaining long-term growth requires strategic planning, adaptability, and ongoing investment in relationships, resources,
and innovation. Whether for organizations, communities, or individuals,
the ability to stay resilient, continue learning, and make adjustments in
response to changing conditions is crucial for lasting success. The continuous cycle of improvement, coupled with a long-term vision, ensures that
growth is not only sustained but also becomes a source of greater impact,
stability, and opportunity over time.

Reflection, Adaptation, and Continuous Growth

Reflection, adaptation, and continuous growth are integral elements of
long-term success, whether in personal development, business, education,
or any other area of life. By consistently reflecting on past experiences,
adapting strategies in response to changing circumstances, and committing to ongoing growth, individuals and organizations can achieve sustained progress and overcome challenges that may arise along the way.

Reflection is a powerful tool for understanding what works and what
doesn't. It allows individuals and organizations to assess past efforts, learn
from mistakes, and celebrate successes. In business, for example, companies that regularly reflect on their performance—through internal reviews, customer feedback, or performance evaluations—can identify areas

of strength and areas that need improvement. A company that reviews its marketing campaigns, for instance, might recognize that certain strategies yielded better results than others, prompting them to adjust future campaigns accordingly. Reflection offers the opportunity to recalibrate and ensure that efforts align with broader goals, keeping growth on track.

Adaptation is the next crucial step in this process. It involves being flexible and open to change in response to new information, shifting priorities, or evolving circumstances. For instance, businesses must constantly adapt to market shifts, consumer preferences, and technological advancements. A good example of adaptation is the way retail companies embraced e-commerce during the rise of online shopping. Many traditional brick-and-mortar stores were initially slow to adapt, but those that successfully pivoted to an online model were able to maintain or even increase their growth. This ability to adapt to new circumstances—whether it's through innovation, diversification, or changing operational strategies—ensures that growth remains viable in an ever-changing world.

Continuous growth is the culmination of reflection and adaptation. It's about viewing success as an ongoing journey rather than a fixed destination. For organizations, continuous growth is driven by a commitment to innovation, learning, and improving processes. In education, schools that embrace continuous growth foster an environment where both teachers and students are encouraged to keep learning. Teachers who engage in professional development, try new teaching methods, and reflect on student outcomes ensure that they remain effective educators who can adapt to the changing needs of their students. Similarly, students who view learning as a lifelong endeavor and are encouraged to seek knowledge beyond the classroom are better equipped to succeed in an ever-changing world.

For example, in the field of technology, continuous growth is essential for staying competitive. Tech companies are constantly evolving their products to meet customer demands and integrate the latest innovations. An example of this can be seen in the development of smartphones, where companies release updated versions with new features each year to adapt to changing consumer needs. By constantly refining their products, these companies stay ahead of competitors and ensure continued growth.

The process of continuous growth also involves building resilience. When faced with setbacks or challenges, individuals and organizations that embrace reflection and adaptation are more likely to bounce back stronger. For instance, a nonprofit organization that experiences a drop in donations may reflect on their fundraising strategies, adapt by diversifying their funding sources, and continue to grow by engaging new supporters. Similarly, an entrepreneur facing a business failure may use the experience as a learning opportunity, adjust their business model, and try again with new insights gained from past mistakes. Resilience is a key part of continuous growth, as it enables individuals and organizations to turn challenges into stepping stones for future success.

In personal relationships, the principles of reflection, adaptation, and growth are also vital. Strong relationships are built on open communication, empathy, and mutual understanding. Individuals who take time to reflect on their interactions, adapt their behaviors based on the needs of others, and strive to improve their communication are more likely to experience sustained, healthy relationships. For example, couples who reflect on their communication patterns, identify areas where they may not be meeting each other's needs, and make conscious adjustments can strengthen their bond over time.

Ultimately, the combination of reflection, adaptation, and continuous growth creates a cycle of ongoing improvement. Each step builds upon the other, ensuring that progress remains steady and sustainable. Whether for a business, a community, or an individual, this approach leads to deeper insights, more effective strategies, and a stronger capacity to thrive in the face of challenges. By committing to this process, individuals and organizations can not only achieve their goals but also continue to evolve in response to new opportunities and obstacles, ensuring that growth is not only sustained but also expanded over time.

In conclusion, embracing reflection, adaptation, and continuous growth is essential for long-term success. These principles help individuals and organizations learn from their experiences, adjust to changing circumstances, and maintain a trajectory of improvement. By consistently assessing progress, being flexible in the face of change, and committing to ongoing development, people and organizations can achieve lasting growth and navigate the complexities of an ever-evolving world.

CHAPTER 10

Personal Development Through the Give–Get–Grow Cycle

Personal development through the *give–get–grow* cycle is a dynamic and powerful process that emphasizes mutual benefit and continuous improvement. At its core, this cycle involves giving, receiving, and growing, with each stage reinforcing the others. It is an approach that encourages individuals to contribute their time, knowledge, and resources to others, in return gaining insights, skills, and opportunities that propel their own growth. This cycle is not only about individual advancement but also about fostering a sense of interconnectedness and reciprocity that benefits both the giver and the receiver.

An example of how this cycle works in personal development can be seen in the context of mentorship. A more experienced individual may give their time and expertise to help a mentee navigate their career, offering guidance, advice, and support. In this case, the mentor is giving of themselves, sharing knowledge and experience. However, the mentor also benefits from this relationship—by teaching others, they deepen their own understanding of their field, gain new perspectives, and develop leadership skills. Moreover, the act of mentoring can be a rewarding experience that boosts the mentor's own sense of fulfillment and purpose.

For the mentee, the act of receiving guidance allows them to grow in their own career, making informed decisions, avoiding common pitfalls, and acquiring valuable insights they may not have otherwise had access to. Through this process of give and get, both parties experience growth. The mentor grows through the act of teaching and reflecting, while the mentee grows through the guidance and knowledge they receive. Over time, the mentee may even become a mentor themselves, continuing the cycle by giving back to others, thus perpetuating the *give–get–grow* cycle.

Another example of this cycle can be found in the world of professional networking. In a networking environment, individuals often give first, whether it's by offering a helping hand, sharing resources, or introducing others to valuable contacts. This is the "give" phase. As a result, they may receive opportunities, knowledge, or connections in return— perhaps a new job lead, advice on how to solve a particular problem, or an invitation to an exclusive event. These new opportunities allow the individual to grow, expanding their network, increasing their skill set, and opening up new avenues for success. By continuously participating in this cycle of giving and receiving, the individual's professional development accelerates, and their career trajectory improves.

In the realm of skill acquisition, the *give–get–grow* cycle can be seen in the context of teaching and learning. A person who volunteers to teach a skill—such as a language, music, or a craft—gives their time, energy, and knowledge to help others learn. This act of teaching allows them to reinforce their own understanding of the subject, identify areas for improvement, and develop new teaching techniques. In return, the students gain valuable skills or knowledge, which leads to their own personal growth. This cycle continues as both the teacher and the students evolve, with the teacher possibly expanding their expertise further and the students applying what they've learned to new challenges.

The *give–get–grow* cycle also operates within a broader societal context. For instance, an individual involved in a volunteer project, such as cleaning up a local park or helping at a food bank, is giving their time and effort to benefit the community. Through this act of giving, the individual experiences personal growth by developing a sense of purpose, enhancing their empathy, and building valuable skills such as teamwork and leadership. At the same time, the community benefits from the volunteer's contributions, creating a virtuous cycle that ultimately fosters growth for both the individual and the community.

Personal development through the *give–get–grow* cycle is not limited to external interactions but can also apply internally. For example, an individual might decide to invest time in self-reflection or journaling. The act of self-reflection—giving time and thought to one's emotions, goals, and experiences—leads to greater self-awareness and insight. As they reflect on their thoughts and feelings, they "get" a deeper understanding of themselves, which allows for personal growth. This self-awareness might inspire changes in behavior or mindset, resulting in improved decision making, emotional intelligence, and overall well-being. The more an individual engages in this process of giving to themselves through self-reflection, the more they grow and evolve.

Overall, the *give–get–grow* cycle in personal development emphasizes the power of reciprocity and mutual benefit. Whether it's through mentorship, professional networking, teaching, or personal reflection, this cycle enables individuals to contribute to others' growth while also receiving valuable experiences and insights that promote their own development. By continuing to give, get, and grow, individuals can create a sustainable path to personal fulfillment, lifelong learning, and success. This cycle reinforces the idea that personal growth is a continuous, reciprocal process that benefits not only the individual but also the broader community they are part of.

The Power of Giving: Strengthening Self and Others

The power of giving is a transformative force that benefits both the giver and the recipient. When individuals give, whether it is their time, resources, or emotional support, they not only contribute to the well-being of others but also experience personal growth and fulfillment. Giving strengthens relationships, enhances personal growth, and creates a ripple effect that can lead to a broader positive impact in communities and societies.

One of the most significant aspects of giving is the way it strengthens the giver. For example, when someone volunteers their time to support a charitable cause, they gain a sense of purpose and satisfaction that is hard to replicate in other areas of life. The act of helping others can boost one's self-esteem, promote feelings of gratitude, and foster a deeper sense of connection with others. Volunteers who regularly contribute to their communities often report feeling more connected to their surroundings and experience increased happiness. A person who volunteers at a food bank, for instance, not only provides essential resources to those in need but also gains perspective on their own life, learning to appreciate what they have. This sense of gratitude often leads to further positive actions and a deeper connection to both self and others.

Giving can also lead to personal growth in terms of emotional intelligence. When individuals offer support to others, especially during difficult times, they develop a greater capacity for empathy and understanding. For example, a mentor who takes the time to guide and support a younger individual through their career journey often gains new insights into leadership, patience, and communication. The act of giving advice, encouragement, or just a listening ear helps the mentor to better understand their own emotional needs and those of others. This empathy-building strengthens their own emotional resilience and makes them more capable of handling challenging situations in their personal and professional lives.

Moreover, giving can lead to a deep sense of fulfillment. This is particularly evident when people engage in acts of kindness that don't require recognition or reward. For example, anonymous donations to charity, helping a neighbor with groceries, or offering a kind word to someone in need can create a powerful sense of fulfillment in the giver. This sense of satisfaction often comes from knowing that one's actions have had a positive effect on someone else's life. The psychological reward that comes from giving—often referred to as the "helper's high"—has been shown to improve mental health, reduce stress, and even increase longevity. Individuals who consistently engage in acts of giving report higher levels of happiness and a sense of well-being, suggesting that giving is an essential part of living a fulfilling life.

In professional settings, giving also plays a key role in strengthening teamwork and collaboration. For example, in a workplace, an employee who offers assistance to a colleague, shares knowledge, or mentors a junior staff member contributes to a culture of collaboration and mutual support. These acts of giving can improve the overall work environment, increase productivity, and build a positive organizational culture. When employees feel supported and valued, they are more likely to engage in reciprocal acts of kindness, creating a virtuous cycle that enhances the effectiveness of the team. A leader who gives their time and attention to help employees develop their skills fosters loyalty and boosts morale, which in turn leads to better performance and job satisfaction.

The power of giving extends beyond personal relationships and into community-building efforts. For example, community leaders who invest time and effort into organizing events, providing resources, or offering guidance help to create stronger, more resilient communities. When people give to one another within a community, whether it's through supporting local businesses, sharing resources, or working together on neighborhood projects, they build a stronger social fabric. This sense of community solidarity can have long-lasting effects, from improved local infrastructure to increased social capital and a better quality of life for all members.

Giving can also strengthen societal bonds at a larger scale. For instance, many organizations and social movements are built around the principle of collective giving. Charitable organizations, advocacy groups, and grassroots initiatives often thrive because people come together to contribute their time, money, or expertise to a cause. The combined efforts of many individuals working toward a common goal can result in significant social change. Whether it's fighting for environmental justice, advocating for human rights, or working to alleviate poverty, the collective power of giving can change the course of history. Individuals who participate in these movements often find themselves growing as people—learning about the issues at hand, meeting others with similar passions, and experiencing the satisfaction of making a tangible difference in the world.

The power of giving is a fundamental driver of both personal and collective growth. Whether it's through small daily acts of kindness or large-scale contributions to causes and communities, giving strengthens the giver by enhancing emotional intelligence, building relationships, and increasing fulfillment. It also creates a ripple effect that strengthens others and fosters positive change. In this way, giving is not only a powerful tool for personal development but also a cornerstone of thriving relationships, strong communities, and a better society. Through giving, individuals find meaning, connection, and growth, which in turn helps them contribute even more to the well-being of others.

The Power of Receiving: Opening Yourself to Growth

The power of getting—whether it's receiving feedback, opportunities, resources, or support—is an essential aspect of personal growth. Opening yourself to receiving can be transformative, helping you expand your horizons, overcome challenges, and realize your potential. Just as giving enriches others, getting allows you to learn, adapt, and grow by providing the tools, insights, and encouragement needed to take the next step forward in your development.

One of the most powerful ways to experience growth through getting is by being open to feedback. In personal and professional contexts, receiving constructive feedback from others can be a catalyst for improvement. For instance, a musician might get feedback from a mentor or colleague about their technique or performance, which can help them refine their skills. A person receiving feedback in a work setting may discover areas where they can enhance their communication, leadership, or problem-solving abilities. This feedback, when approached with an open mind, provides valuable insights that can help individuals recognize blind spots, avoid repeating mistakes, and improve their overall performance. The process of getting feedback not only helps individuals grow in their current roles but also prepares them for future challenges.

Similarly, getting new experiences or exposure to different perspectives is another way to open yourself to growth. Traveling, meeting people from diverse backgrounds, or engaging with new ideas can expand your worldview and stimulate personal growth. For example, someone who has worked in one industry for years might transition into a new field and get the opportunity to learn from experts in that industry. By absorbing new knowledge, adapting to new environments, and engaging with fresh ideas, they can build new skills and broaden their capacity for innovation. This kind of exposure to new experiences challenges preconceived notions and forces individuals to stretch their thinking and adapt in ways that foster growth.

Receiving mentorship is another powerful form of getting that accelerates personal development. When you open yourself to guidance from a mentor, you tap into the experience and wisdom of someone who has walked the path before you. This relationship not only provides direction but also offers reassurance during times of uncertainty. For example, an aspiring entrepreneur might seek out a mentor who has successfully launched businesses, learning from their successes and failures. The mentor's insights and advice can guide the mentee through challenges and help them avoid common pitfalls. In turn, the mentee's growth is enhanced because they are able to leverage the mentor's experience, ultimately reaching their own potential faster than they might have on their own. This process of getting mentorship not only benefits the mentee but also deepens the mentor's own understanding, as teaching and guiding others is often a powerful learning experience.

Opportunities for getting can also be found in everyday interactions. A colleague may offer assistance on a project, or a friend might provide emotional support during a difficult time. The act of accepting help, whether it's in the form of assistance, advice, or emotional support, encourages a sense of community and connection. It opens individuals to vulnerability, allowing them to see that growth often requires collaboration and support from others. For example, someone who has always been independent may face a personal crisis and allow friends and family to help them. Through this experience, they not only receive the support they need but also learn the value of relying on others and accepting that they don't have to do everything alone.

Getting also plays a central role in the acquisition of knowledge and skills. Whether it's enrolling in a course, reading books, or watching instructional videos, learning new things opens up opportunities for personal growth. For example, someone who is looking to change careers might get the opportunity to take a coding boot camp. As they learn new programming languages and skills, they expand their professional abilities and increase their marketability in the job market. This new knowledge creates a foundation for future opportunities and personal growth, allowing them to take steps toward a more fulfilling career.

On a personal level, getting can also relate to self-care and mental well-being. Opening yourself to getting help, whether through therapy, counseling, or simply talking to a friend about personal struggles, is an essential part of emotional growth. Many individuals, particularly those who are accustomed to managing their challenges alone, may hesitate to seek help. However, getting assistance during times of stress or difficulty can be transformative. Whether it's receiving guidance on coping strategies or simply having someone listen, these experiences allow individuals to process their emotions, gain new insights, and build emotional resilience. Through these interactions, individuals often learn that growth is not just about pushing forward alone but also about recognizing when to reach out for support and what that support can bring.

Getting is also a key component of self-reflection and internal growth. Sometimes, opening oneself to growth means accepting and understanding one's own emotions, thoughts, and experiences. For instance, a person who practices journaling or mindfulness might "get" new insights about their behaviors, motivations, and desires. Through this internal process, they can identify areas for improvement, challenge unproductive habits, and set new personal goals. This introspective process helps individuals make informed decisions, align their actions with their values, and build a stronger sense of self.

In the broader context of societal growth, the power of getting is evident in how individuals and communities come together to support each other in times of need. After a natural disaster, for example, affected communities may receive aid in the form of food, shelter, and medical care. In these situations, the act of getting is crucial for survival and recovery. However, it also has a broader impact on long-term growth. The support received during a crisis fosters a sense of solidarity and can inspire individuals to give back in the future, contributing to the overall resilience of the community. This cycle of getting and giving strengthens collective bonds and promotes future growth.

The power of getting, then, is about recognizing the opportunities for growth that come from receiving support, knowledge, feedback, and experiences. By being open to what others offer, whether it's guidance, resources, or assistance, individuals create the conditions necessary for their own growth. In doing so, they cultivate a deeper understanding of themselves, develop new skills, and open doors to opportunities that would not be accessible without receiving. Embracing the power of getting not only contributes to personal development but also fosters a broader sense of connection and collaboration that benefits everyone involved.

The Power of Growing: Continuous Learning and Self-improvement

The power of growing through continuous learning and self-improvement is at the heart of personal development. Growth is not a destination but an ongoing journey that involves a commitment to constantly evolving, adapting, and refining oneself. This process of growth encourages individuals to seek new knowledge, challenge their existing beliefs, and improve their skills to reach their fullest potential. By embracing a mindset of continuous learning and self-improvement, individuals can unlock their capacity for success, fulfillment, and resilience in an ever-changing world.

A key element of growing is the pursuit of new knowledge. For example, an individual who takes up a new hobby or field of study often experiences personal growth as they acquire new skills and expand their intellectual horizons. Someone who decides to learn a new language is not only gaining the ability to communicate in another language but also developing cognitive abilities, such as problem-solving, memory, and multitasking. This process of learning exposes the learner to different ways of thinking and enhances their adaptability. Over time, this new knowledge can lead to greater opportunities, from career advancement to enriching personal experiences.

In the workplace, the power of growing through continuous learning can have a significant impact on career progression. For instance, an employee who regularly seeks out professional development opportunities—whether through workshops, online courses, or conferences—demonstrates a commitment to growth. By acquiring new skills and staying updated on industry trends, they enhance their value to the organization and increase their potential for promotion. Additionally, this ongoing learning enables individuals to take on more challenging and diverse responsibilities, which fosters further growth. For example, someone who learns project management skills might be given the opportunity to lead a team, providing them with hands-on experience and a chance to develop leadership qualities.

Self-improvement also involves the refinement of existing skills and behaviors. A person who recognizes areas in their life that could benefit from growth—such as emotional intelligence, communication, or time management—can focus on improving these aspects. For example, someone who struggles with managing their time effectively might invest in learning techniques for better organization, such as time-blocking or using productivity apps. Over time, these improvements lead to greater efficiency, reduced stress, and a sense of accomplishment. In personal relationships, individuals who work on improving their communication skills, whether through active listening or expressing themselves more clearly, often see stronger, more fulfilling connections with others. Self-improvement in this way helps individuals achieve a higher quality of life, both personally and professionally.

Growth through continuous learning is not limited to acquiring new skills; it also involves cultivating a mindset that is open to change and innovation. For example, an individual who embraces the concept of "growth mindset"—the belief that abilities and intelligence can be developed through effort and learning—approaches challenges with resilience and curiosity. Instead of seeing failure as a setback, they view it as an opportunity to learn and grow. This mindset fosters a willingness to step outside one's comfort zone and take risks. A person who applies this mindset might decide to change careers later in life, knowing that they can learn the necessary skills and adapt to the new role. This adaptability and openness to change are crucial in today's rapidly evolving world, where new technologies, industries, and opportunities are constantly emerging.

Growth also occurs through the process of reflection and self-awareness. Individuals who take time to reflect on their experiences, values, and goals can gain valuable insights into their personal development. For example, someone who journals regularly or practices mindfulness might reflect on their emotional responses to various situations, learning to understand why they react in certain ways and how to manage their emotions better. This reflective process fosters greater self-awareness, which is a key driver of growth. Through reflection, individuals can identify their strengths and weaknesses, set more meaningful goals, and make more informed decisions. Over time, this self-awareness leads to a more balanced and purposeful life, as individuals align their actions with their values and aspirations.

In terms of personal relationships, the power of growing through continuous learning and self-improvement can also be seen in how people adapt and evolve with others. Relationships are dynamic, and growth within them requires ongoing effort. For example, a couple that has been together for several years may go through periods where they face challenges in communication or understanding each other's needs. However, by committing to personal growth—such as improving communication skills, being more empathetic, or learning conflict resolution strategies—the couple can grow together, strengthening their bond and creating a deeper, more resilient relationship. Similarly, a parent might engage in personal growth to better understand their child's developmental needs, allowing them to adapt their parenting approach as the child matures.

An important aspect of growth is the ability to overcome adversity. Personal growth often occurs during times of hardship, as individuals learn how to navigate difficult circumstances and emerge stronger. For example, someone who faces a personal loss or significant challenge may experience a period of emotional struggle but, through resilience and self-reflection, may ultimately come to see the experience as an opportunity for growth. They may learn new coping strategies, develop a greater sense of empathy, and deepen their understanding of what truly matters in life. In this way, growth is not just about accumulating knowledge or skills but also about developing the inner strength to face and overcome challenges.

Growth through continuous learning and self-improvement is a lifelong process that requires dedication, openness, and a willingness to change. Whether through acquiring new knowledge, refining existing skills, embracing a growth mindset, or learning from adversity, personal growth enriches every aspect of life. The more individuals invest in their own growth, the more they unlock their potential for success, fulfillment, and resilience. This ongoing cycle of learning, adapting, and improving creates a foundation for lasting personal transformation, allowing individuals to live more purposeful, meaningful lives.

The Synergy Between Personal Development and Community Growth

The synergy between personal development and community growth is a powerful and transformative force. When individuals focus on their own growth and development, they not only enhance their own lives but also contribute to the betterment of the communities they are a part of. Similarly, strong communities provide the support, encouragement, and resources that individuals need to thrive. This reciprocal relationship between personal and community growth creates a virtuous cycle where both individuals and their communities become stronger and more resilient over time.

One of the most significant ways that personal development contributes to community growth is through the creation of positive role models. As individuals improve themselves, they often inspire others around them to do the same. For example, someone who overcomes adversity, such as financial hardship or a difficult personal situation, can become a source of inspiration for others facing similar challenges. By demonstrating resilience and a commitment to personal growth, they show others that transformation is possible, motivating them to take steps toward their own development. This ripple effect of personal growth can create a culture of improvement within a community, where people are more likely to support each other and work together to overcome collective challenges.

In a community setting, individuals who engage in personal development often bring new skills, knowledge, and perspectives that benefit the broader group. For instance, an individual who invests time in learning leadership or conflict resolution skills can play a crucial role in resolving disputes within their community or leading initiatives that bring people together. These individuals can become agents of change, helping to foster unity and cooperation. For example, a community leader who continuously works on their communication skills, empathy, and understanding of diverse perspectives is better equipped to mediate conflicts and build strong, cohesive groups. Their growth as a leader directly benefits the community, promoting collaboration, problem-solving, and collective action.

The synergy between personal development and community growth can also be seen in how individuals contribute to social causes. Personal growth often leads to a deeper sense of purpose and a desire to make a positive impact on the world. Someone who develops greater empathy, for example, might become involved in volunteering or advocacy, addressing issues like poverty, homelessness, or environmental sustainability. By participating in community service or social change initiatives, they contribute their time, energy, and talents to improving their surroundings. At the same time, their involvement in these causes can deepen their personal sense of fulfillment, expand their social networks, and enhance their skills. This dual benefit—personal growth through giving and community growth through collective action—strengthens the bond between individuals and their communities.

Moreover, as individuals grow in their personal lives, they are often better equipped to contribute to the economic, cultural, and social fabric of their communities. For instance, someone who develops strong business acumen and entrepreneurial skills can start a business that provides jobs and services to the local community. Through their success, they not only improve their own financial situation but also create opportunities for others, fueling local economic growth. A successful business owner may also contribute to their community by supporting local charities, sponsoring events, or mentoring aspiring entrepreneurs. In this way, personal development directly contributes to the broader community's prosperity and well-being.

The growth of individuals also leads to stronger social networks and connections within communities. As people work on their own personal growth, they often become more engaged in community activities, forming deeper relationships with others who share similar values and goals. This sense of connection fosters trust, cooperation, and mutual support, which are key elements of a thriving community. For example, when individuals invest in developing their communication and leadership skills, they are better able to engage with others in a positive and constructive way. This leads to stronger social bonds and creates a sense of belonging that strengthens the community as a whole.

Additionally, personal development can foster a greater sense of responsibility toward the community. As individuals grow in their understanding of themselves and the world around them, they often become more aware of the issues and challenges facing their communities. This awareness can inspire them to take action, whether by participating in local governance, organizing community initiatives, or advocating for policy changes. By taking responsibility for their role within the community, individuals contribute to creating a more inclusive, supportive, and sustainable environment for everyone. For example, someone who becomes aware of environmental issues may take steps to reduce their carbon footprint, educate others, or advocate for greener practices in their community.

In this way, the synergy between personal development and community growth creates a dynamic cycle of mutual reinforcement. Personal development strengthens individuals, who in turn contribute to the growth and resilience of their communities. At the same time, strong communities provide the resources, support, and opportunities that allow individuals to thrive. This interconnected relationship helps create an environment where both personal and collective growth are not only possible but encouraged. Communities that support personal development foster a sense of belonging, empowerment, and shared purpose, while individuals who invest in their own growth become catalysts for positive change and progress within their communities. This synergy ultimately leads to more vibrant, resilient, and thriving communities where individuals and groups are continually evolving and improving together.

The Continuous Cycle of *Give–Get–Grow*

The continuous cycle of *give–get–grow* is an ongoing process that reinforces itself, creating a dynamic environment for personal and collective development. At its core, this cycle revolves around the idea that giving leads to receiving, which in turn fuels further growth. This interplay between giving, receiving, and growing builds momentum, benefiting not only individuals but also the communities they are part of. The power of this cycle lies in its ability to foster a sense of purpose, connection, and continuous improvement, creating positive outcomes on both personal and communal levels.

When individuals engage in giving, whether through their time, skills, resources, or knowledge, they contribute to the betterment of their communities. For instance, volunteering to mentor others, sharing expertise, or participating in charitable causes all represent forms of giving. In doing so, individuals help others meet their needs, build connections, and foster a sense of community. This act of giving often leads to receiving in various forms. Giving can result in receiving support, respect, gratitude, or new opportunities. A mentor who shares their knowledge with a younger individual might receive the satisfaction of seeing their mentee succeed, as well as the joy of fostering a connection. Moreover, the mentor may also learn from their mentee's fresh perspectives, creating a mutually beneficial dynamic.

The act of receiving is an important part of the cycle, as it enables growth. By being open to receiving, individuals allow themselves to gain insights, feedback, and resources that are essential for personal development. For example, a person who gives their time and energy to a community project might receive support and recognition in return. This encouragement can help them develop new skills or strengthen existing ones, such as teamwork, leadership, or problem-solving. In a workplace setting, someone who contributes to a team's success might receive constructive feedback or professional development opportunities, further enhancing their growth potential. By receiving, individuals are not only recognizing the value of what is offered to them but also creating an environment where continued exchange leads to long-term development.

Once an individual has received, they are positioned to grow—both personally and professionally. Growth is the natural outcome of giving and receiving, as it allows individuals to build on their experiences and continue evolving. The skills, knowledge, and relationships gained through giving and receiving catalyze further development. For instance, a leader who provides guidance and support to their team members may experience personal growth by developing their leadership qualities and emotional intelligence. At the same time, the team members benefit from the leader's mentorship and are empowered to take on new challenges. This growth not only enhances the individual's capabilities but also strengthens the entire team, creating a culture of continuous improvement.

The process of growing, in turn, leads to more giving. As individuals grow and expand their capabilities, they become better equipped to contribute to the development of others. This creates a cycle where giving, receiving, and growth feed into one another. For example, a person who has grown in their career and gained expertise in a particular field may choose to give back by mentoring others, contributing to industry knowledge, or supporting community projects. As they give, they are also likely to receive new opportunities, perspectives, or recognition, which fuels further growth. The more individuals grow, the more they can contribute, leading to a cycle of continuous learning, support, and community development.

The *give–get–grow* cycle is also essential for fostering a culture of collaboration and resilience. In communities where individuals are committed to giving, receiving, and growing together, the collective strength of the group increases. For example, in a workplace where employees actively share knowledge, offer support to one another, and continuously strive for personal development, the organization as a whole benefits. The synergy between individual growth and collective growth strengthens the organization's culture, increases its adaptability, and enhances its capacity to achieve long-term goals. Similarly, in a community setting, people who are invested in giving back, learning from each other, and growing together create a more resilient and empowered community. Whether through sharing resources, supporting one another during times of need, or collectively working toward common goals, communities that embrace the *give–get–grow* cycle are better equipped to navigate challenges and thrive in the face of adversity.

The *give–get–grow* cycle also has a long-term impact on social change. When individuals and communities embrace this cycle, they contribute to broader societal improvements. A person who grows in their understanding of social issues, for instance, may decide to give their time and resources to causes that address inequality, poverty, or environmental sustainability. As they engage with others who are similarly invested in social change, they both receive new insights and feedback that fuel their continued growth. Over time, these collective efforts can lead to significant positive changes within society, as individuals and communities come together to create a more just, equitable, and sustainable world.

In conclusion, the *give–get–grow* cycle is a continuous, interconnected process that drives personal development, strengthens communities, and fosters social change. By embracing the dynamics of giving, receiving, and growing, individuals create positive momentum that leads to lasting transformation, both within themselves and in the world around them. The beauty of this cycle lies in its ability to perpetuate itself—each act of giving is met with the potential for receiving, which in turn fuels further growth. This cyclical process of development creates a foundation for individuals and communities to thrive, ensuring that growth is sustained and shared, resulting in a more vibrant, supportive, and resilient society.

CHAPTER 11

Leadership in the *Give–Get–Grow* Cycle

Leadership in the *give–get–grow* cycle plays a crucial role in shaping both personal and collective development within organizations and communities. Leaders who embrace this cycle foster environments where individuals feel empowered to give their time, skills, and resources while also being open to receiving support, feedback, and new opportunities. In doing so, they create a culture of growth that extends beyond individual development to benefit the entire group or community. Through effective leadership, the principles of giving, receiving, and growing become interconnected, driving positive change and long-term success.

One of the ways leadership influences the *give–get–grow* cycle is by modeling the behavior of giving. Leaders who actively invest in their teams and communities by sharing their knowledge, offering guidance, and providing resources set the tone for others to follow. For instance, a leader who takes time to mentor a new employee or volunteer their expertise in a community project demonstrates the importance of giving to others. This act of giving can inspire team members or community members to also offer their support, whether through sharing skills, providing encouragement, or contributing to a shared goal. The ripple effect of this giving behavior spreads throughout the group, strengthening relationships and fostering a collaborative atmosphere.

As leaders give, they also encourage others to be open to receiving. The act of receiving, whether it's feedback, constructive criticism, or new learning opportunities, is essential for growth. A good leader understands that growth cannot occur in isolation and that receiving is just as important as giving. For example, a leader who actively seeks feedback from their team members shows vulnerability and a commitment to continuous improvement. This willingness to receive feedback not only helps the leader grow but also sets a positive example for others. It encourages team members to be open to feedback and new ideas, knowing that the goal is collective growth rather than individual success. Leaders who create a safe space for open communication and feedback build trust, helping individuals feel more comfortable in seeking and receiving support.

Leaders who embrace the *give–get–grow* cycle also recognize that growth is a mutual process. They understand that by helping others grow, they are also growing themselves. This cyclical relationship of giving, receiving, and growing enhances the leader's ability to drive change, innovate, and lead with purpose. For instance, when a leader mentors someone, they not only impart knowledge but also learn from the mentee's experiences and perspectives. This exchange can challenge the leader's thinking, encourage self-reflection, and lead to new insights. As the leader grows, they are better equipped to guide their team or community through challenges and opportunities, fostering an environment where everyone has the chance to grow.

Leadership also plays a key role in creating a culture of collaboration within the *give–get–grow* cycle. Leaders who encourage collaboration and teamwork foster a sense of shared responsibility for success. For example, a leader who promotes a collaborative work environment in which team members share ideas, offer help, and support one another's growth sets the foundation for collective success. In a team-based setting, leaders who emphasize the importance of cooperation and shared goals encourage individuals to give their skills and time for the benefit of the group. As team members receive help from others and grow together, the entire team becomes stronger and more resilient. This collaborative culture reinforces the cycle of giving, receiving, and growing, ultimately leading to greater collective achievements.

In community settings, leadership in the *give–get–grow* cycle can have a transformative impact. Community leaders who encourage individuals to give back—whether through volunteering, sharing expertise, or supporting local initiatives—foster a spirit of generosity and collective well-being. For example, a leader who organizes community outreach programs or social events encourages individuals to contribute their time and energy to improving the community. As people give, they also receive the benefits of strengthened relationships, increased community cohesion, and a sense of shared purpose. Over time, this collective growth strengthens the fabric of the community, leading to a more resilient and connected society.

The impact of leadership in the *give–get–grow* cycle extends beyond short-term results. Leaders who consistently model giving, receiving, and growing create long-lasting change within their teams, organizations, or communities. For example, a leader who nurtures an environment of continuous learning and growth not only improves the skills of those they lead but also enhances the long-term sustainability of the organization or community. By fostering a culture where individuals are encouraged to give and receive, and where personal and collective growth is prioritized, leaders lay the groundwork for future success.

In conclusion, leadership within the *give–get–grow* cycle is fundamental to creating a thriving and sustainable environment, whether in the workplace or in the community. Leaders who actively engage in giving, receiving, and fostering growth not only enhance their own development but also inspire others to do the same. Through their actions and commitment to continuous improvement, leaders create a cycle of mutual benefit that drives personal and collective success. By nurturing this cycle, leaders empower those around them to contribute to positive change, ensuring long-term growth and resilience for both individuals and the broader community.

The Role of Giving in Leadership

The role of giving in leadership is foundational to creating a positive and impactful environment for both individuals and teams. Leaders who prioritize giving—whether through their time, resources, knowledge, or support—set a tone of generosity and selflessness that encourages others to do the same. This act of giving not only strengthens relationships and trust but also fosters a culture of collaboration and collective growth. When leaders give, they cultivate an atmosphere of mutual respect and shared responsibility, which benefits the entire organization or community.

One of the most significant ways that giving plays a role in leadership is by building trust. Trust is a cornerstone of effective leadership, and leaders who demonstrate their willingness to give are often the ones who inspire the trust of their followers. For example, a leader who takes the time to listen to their team members' concerns, provides guidance, or offers support during difficult times shows that they care about the well-being of others. By giving of their time and attention, they build a deeper connection with their team, which can enhance cooperation and collaboration. In turn, team members are more likely to reciprocate, giving their best effort in return, creating a cycle of trust and support that strengthens the overall dynamic.

In leadership, giving also plays a critical role in fostering a sense of unity and collaboration within teams. When a leader shares credit for successes, acknowledges the contributions of others, or provides support to overcome obstacles, it reinforces the idea that success is a collective effort. For example, a leader who recognizes the hard work of team members in achieving a goal, whether through public praise or private acknowledgment, shows that they value the contributions of others. This not only boosts morale but also encourages others to continue giving their best effort, knowing that their work is appreciated. Leaders who give credit where it's due create a culture of collaboration, where everyone feels valued and motivated to contribute to the team's success.

Another key aspect of giving in leadership is the ability to provide emotional support. Leadership is not just about guiding people through tasks and challenges; it is also about supporting them through personal and emotional difficulties. For instance, a leader who checks in on their team members' well-being during stressful periods, offers encouragement, or provides flexibility during tough times helps to build a resilient and loyal team. This type of giving—emotional support—fosters a sense of belonging and connection, making team members feel that they are not just employees but valued individuals. In a workplace where leaders are attuned to the emotional needs of their team, members are more likely to feel motivated and committed, which increases both individual and organizational performance.

Giving also helps leaders to develop a deeper understanding of their teams. When leaders take the time to give—whether through mentoring, actively listening, or helping team members overcome challenges— they gain insight into the needs, strengths, and potential of their team. This insight allows them to better align resources, create opportunities for growth, and make decisions that benefit the team and organization. For example, a leader who spends time getting to know their employees' skills and aspirations can tailor development opportunities to help each individual reach their full potential. This personal investment not only enhances the performance of the team but also fosters loyalty, as team members feel that their leader genuinely cares about their growth and success.

Furthermore, giving in leadership can drive innovation and problem-solving. Leaders who create an environment where giving is encouraged—such as sharing ideas, offering feedback, or collaborating on projects—foster a culture of creativity and innovation. For instance, a leader who encourages open dialogue and values the input of all team members creates an atmosphere where new ideas can flourish. When leaders give space for others to contribute and express their ideas, it leads to more diverse solutions and creative approaches to challenges. A leader who is willing to give the floor to their team, ask for suggestions, and incorporate feedback is more likely to inspire a collaborative approach to problem-solving. This environment of open exchange allows the team to collectively develop innovative solutions that may not have emerged in a more hierarchical or rigid structure.

Giving in leadership is also about serving others, especially in the context of servant leadership. Servant leadership is a philosophy where the leader's primary role is to serve and support others, rather than to dominate or control. A servant leader focuses on the growth and well-being of their team members and ensures that their needs are met. This could involve offering professional development opportunities, advocating for the team's needs within the organization, or being available to listen and provide guidance when needed. For example, a leader who provides resources for team members to pursue continuing education or who supports work–life balance initiatives is giving back to the team in a meaningful way. By putting the needs of others first, servant leaders create an environment where individuals feel valued, and this sense of value can translate into increased loyalty, job satisfaction, and productivity.

Giving also contributes to the development of a leader's own character. As leaders engage in acts of service and selflessness, they develop humility, empathy, and emotional intelligence—qualities that are essential for effective leadership. By continuously giving of their time, energy, and resources, leaders learn to prioritize others' needs, communicate effectively, and maintain a long-term vision for the success of their team. For example, a leader who gives feedback in a constructive and supportive manner not only helps their team grow but also demonstrates their commitment to personal growth and development as a leader. This continuous process of giving and learning can help leaders evolve into more compassionate, empathetic, and effective individuals, which ultimately benefits both their personal growth and the success of their teams.

In conclusion, giving is an integral part of leadership that impacts both the leader and the team they lead. By prioritizing giving—whether through sharing knowledge, offering emotional support, providing mentorship, or fostering collaboration—leaders create environments where individuals feel valued, supported, and empowered. This act of giving strengthens relationships, builds trust, and drives both personal and collective growth. Leaders who consistently give to their teams not only cultivate an atmosphere of collaboration and mutual respect but also inspire others to contribute to the success of the group. Ultimately, leadership rooted in the principle of giving promotes long-term growth, strengthens communities, and drives sustainable success.

The Role of Getting in Leadership

The role of getting in leadership is often overlooked, yet it is essential for leaders to be open to receiving in order to foster growth, improve their leadership capabilities, and build stronger relationships with their teams. Just as giving is vital in leadership, getting—whether it be feedback, support, resources, or ideas—plays a crucial role in a leader's development and the success of the organization. Effective leaders understand that they cannot lead in isolation and that being receptive to getting help helps them grow, learn, and adapt to the needs of their teams and environments.

One of the most important aspects of getting in leadership is being open to feedback. A leader who actively seeks and receives feedback, whether from their team, peers, or mentors, demonstrates humility and a willingness to improve. For example, a leader who asks their team members for constructive criticism on their leadership style or decision-making process shows that they value input from others and are committed to becoming better. This openness to feedback not only helps the leader make more informed decisions but also builds trust within the team. When team members see that their feedback is valued and acted upon, they are more likely to engage, feel respected, and contribute more actively to the team's goals. In this way, the leader's openness to getting feedback creates a more transparent and collaborative work environment.

Getting also involves receiving support from others, which is critical for a leader's success. Leadership can be isolating at times, and no leader can carry out their responsibilities without assistance from others. A leader who is able to ask for help, delegate tasks, and rely on their team's expertise demonstrates both trust and recognition of others' strengths. For example, a leader who recognizes when they need help with a project or decision and actively seeks input from their team can leverage the diverse skills and perspectives within the group. This allows the leader to make better-informed choices and ensures that the team feels valued for their contributions. By getting the support they need, leaders not only enhance their own effectiveness but also empower their team members, who feel they are an essential part of the leadership process.

Leaders also benefit from getting emotional support. Leadership can be stressful, and having a network of trusted individuals who offer encouragement, understanding, and advice is vital. A leader who is open to receiving emotional support, whether from friends, mentors, or peers, can maintain their resilience and well-being. For example, a leader who faces a difficult decision or a challenging period might turn to a mentor or a peer for advice and emotional encouragement. This support allows the leader to process their thoughts, gain perspective, and approach challenges with a clear mind. The ability to get emotional support when needed not only helps the leader manage stress but also strengthens their emotional intelligence, a key trait for effective leadership.

In the context of teams, getting is just as vital as giving. Leaders who are open to receiving ideas and input from their team members create a more inclusive and innovative work environment. For example, a leader who asks their team for suggestions on improving a process or solving a problem shows that they value the expertise and creativity of their team. When leaders receive ideas from team members, it creates a sense of shared ownership and collective responsibility. This engagement empowers employees, makes them feel invested in the organization's success, and encourages them to contribute their best work. By getting ideas and feedback from their team, leaders can also identify potential issues or opportunities that they may not have seen on their own.

Furthermore, receiving recognition and appreciation plays a critical role in leadership. Leaders who are open to receiving praise or acknowledgment, whether for their decisions, efforts, or accomplishments, help to foster a culture of positivity and mutual respect. While leadership is often about giving credit to others, leaders themselves need to recognize and acknowledge their own achievements. This is not about ego, but about setting a healthy precedent for self-recognition and modeling a balanced approach to feedback. For example, a leader who acknowledges their own successes, whether big or small, alongside acknowledging the contributions of others, reinforces a culture of appreciation and gratitude within the team. This balance allows the team to see that leadership is not a one-way street, and that their contributions, as well as the leader's, are valuable.

Another significant way that getting is critical in leadership is in receiving the right resources to support both personal and team growth. Effective leaders understand that they cannot lead alone; they need the right tools, resources, and support structures to drive success. For instance, a leader who advocates for training opportunities, technological upgrades, or improved team structures is actively seeking resources that will benefit the organization's overall health. By getting the resources they need, leaders ensure that their teams have what they require to be productive, creative, and efficient. This ability to secure resources not only enhances team performance but also builds trust in the leader's ability to advocate for and meet the needs of the team.

In conclusion, the role of getting in leadership is essential for the growth and success of both the leader and their team. A leader who is open to receiving feedback, support, ideas, and resources demonstrates humility, a commitment to continuous improvement, and a dedication to empowering others. The ability to get emotional support, learn from others, and receive recognition not only strengthens the leader's resilience but also fosters a culture of collaboration, innovation, and mutual respect within the team. Leaders who understand the value of getting, alongside giving, create environments that are adaptable, forward-thinking, and continuously evolving—leading to long-term success and growth for both individuals and organizations.

The Role of Growing in Leadership

The role of growing in leadership is fundamental to the success and sustainability of both the leader and the organization. Growth, in the context of leadership, refers to the continuous process of developing skills, gaining new knowledge, adapting to challenges, and improving one's ability to guide and inspire others. Leaders who focus on growing—not only personally but also in how they develop their teams—help foster an environment where learning and improvement are prioritized. Growth in leadership involves both personal growth and the growth of others, as both are essential to creating a thriving, innovative, and successful environment.

One of the primary aspects of growing in leadership is the willingness to evolve and adapt over time. Effective leaders do not remain static in their approach but seek to develop their skills and perspectives continually. For example, a leader who faces a significant organizational change, such as a merger or a restructuring, must be able to grow in their understanding of new systems, processes, and team dynamics. By embracing the challenge and learning how to navigate this transition, the leader can guide their team through the changes smoothly. This kind of growth helps the leader stay relevant in an ever-changing world and ensures they can make informed decisions, manage new challenges, and provide clear guidance to their team.

Growth in leadership also involves developing emotional intelligence—understanding and managing one's own emotions and recognizing and influencing the emotions of others. Leaders with high emotional intelligence can build strong relationships, resolve conflicts effectively, and motivate their teams in ways that foster trust and collaboration. For instance, a leader who practices empathy and actively listens to the concerns of their team can create a safe and supportive work environment. When a leader grows in emotional intelligence, they become more attuned to the needs of their team members, allowing them to provide tailored support and guidance. This, in turn, enhances the team's overall performance and cohesion. A leader who grows emotionally can also better handle stress and setbacks, which are inevitable in leadership roles, and can remain calm and focused in times of crisis, setting an example for others to follow.

Leadership growth is also marked by the continuous pursuit of knowledge and skills. Effective leaders understand that they cannot rely solely on their past experiences or expertise but must constantly seek to improve and stay current with new trends, technologies, and management practices. For example, a leader who attends leadership development workshops, reads books on management and organizational behavior, or seeks out mentors in their field demonstrates a commitment to personal and professional growth. This not only improves the leader's ability to make informed decisions but also sets a positive example for their team. When leaders invest in their own growth, they show their teams that learning is a lifelong endeavor, which encourages a culture of growth and development within the organization. As team members observe their leaders pursuing continuous learning, they are more likely to follow suit and prioritize their own growth, creating a cycle of improvement across the entire organization.

Leadership growth is also tied to the ability to adapt leadership styles to suit the needs of different situations and individuals. One leadership style does not fit all, and effective leaders know when to adjust their approach based on the circumstances. For example, a leader who adapts their style to be more direct during times of crisis, while taking a more collaborative approach during routine operations, demonstrates growth in their leadership abilities. Similarly, leaders who recognize that each team member has different strengths, weaknesses, and learning styles, and adjust their interactions accordingly, help foster an environment where all team members feel valued and empowered to grow. By growing in their understanding of diverse team dynamics and adjusting their approach, leaders can create a more inclusive and productive team environment.

Another important aspect of growing in leadership is developing strategic thinking. Leaders must continuously grow in their ability to think beyond the day-to-day operations and consider long-term goals, potential risks, and opportunities for innovation. A leader who grows in strategic thinking is able to identify emerging trends, anticipate challenges, and make decisions that align with the organization's long-term vision. For instance, a leader who proactively addresses market shifts, technological advancements, or changes in customer expectations can position their organization to adapt and thrive in a competitive landscape. Strategic growth allows leaders to stay ahead of the curve and guide their organizations toward sustained success.

Moreover, growth in leadership often involves expanding one's capacity for resilience. Leaders who grow in their ability to face challenges head-on, recover from setbacks, and inspire others to do the same help to build a resilient organization. For example, a leader who leads their team through a period of financial difficulty or organizational change with optimism and perseverance can instill a sense of resilience in their team. Leaders who grow in resilience are not only better equipped to handle adversity themselves but also teach their teams how to remain focused, motivated, and adaptable during challenging times. This kind of growth is essential for navigating both internal and external pressures and ensuring the long-term stability of the organization.

Leadership growth also requires the development of strong decision-making skills. As leaders face more complex challenges and higher stakes, they must grow in their ability to make sound decisions under pressure. For example, a leader who demonstrates growth in decision making by weighing the pros and cons of different options, consulting with relevant stakeholders, and taking calculated risks can improve the outcomes of their choices. Effective decision making is critical for leaders, as it impacts not only the success of the organization but also the trust and confidence of their teams. As leaders grow in their decision-making abilities, they become more effective in guiding their teams and making choices that align with the organization's values and goals.

In conclusion, growing in leadership is essential for both personal and organizational success. Leaders who focus on growing—not just in terms of their own skills but also in how they help their teams and organizations develop—create a culture of continuous improvement, innovation, and resilience. Growth in leadership involves a commitment to learning, adapting, fostering growth in others, and developing the skills needed to lead effectively. When leaders prioritize their own growth and the growth of those they lead, they pave the way for long-term success and sustainability, both for themselves and their organizations.

Leadership Through the Lens of the *Give–Get–Grow* Cycle

Leadership through the lens of the *give–get–grow* cycle emphasizes the interconnectedness of giving, receiving, and growing within the context of effective leadership. It illustrates that leadership is not just about taking charge, but about creating an environment in which all members of a team contribute, learn, and evolve together. By examining leadership through this cycle, we see how leaders can inspire collaboration, foster mutual respect, and drive both individual and collective growth.

The "give" aspect of leadership refers to how leaders provide support, guidance, resources, and empowerment to their teams. A leader who gives generously creates a foundation of trust and reciprocity. For example, a leader who offers their time to mentor team members, provide constructive feedback, or actively support their career development shows a commitment to their growth. By giving their knowledge, encouragement, and opportunities for professional advancement, leaders enable their teams to reach their potential. A good leader also gives attention to cultivating a positive organizational culture, ensuring that their actions align with the values of respect, inclusivity, and accountability. When leaders give in this way, they not only help their team members succeed but also foster loyalty and commitment within the group. This culture of giving encourages employees to reciprocate by contributing their best work, ideas, and energy to the organization.

The "get" component of the cycle underscores the importance of leaders being open to receiving. Effective leaders understand that leadership is not a one-way street and that they must remain open to receiving feedback, ideas, support, and even criticism from others. Leaders who actively seek input from their teams show that they value diverse perspectives and are willing to learn. For example, a leader who regularly solicits feedback about their leadership style and decision-making process demonstrates humility and a desire to improve. This openness not only helps the leader grow but also empowers team members to take ownership of the process. When employees feel their voices are heard, it builds a sense of trust and respect, and they are more likely to engage actively in achieving the team's goals.

The "grow" phase is where the full potential of leadership is realized. Growth in leadership is not just about personal development, but about fostering growth in others and within the organization as a whole. Leaders who prioritize growth create an environment where continuous learning and improvement are embedded in the culture. Growth happens in various forms: developing new skills, acquiring knowledge, enhancing emotional intelligence, and adapting leadership styles to meet evolving challenges. A leader who prioritizes their own growth through ongoing education, self-reflection, and skill development is better equipped to lead their team through complex and changing circumstances. For example, a leader who stays informed about new industry trends, attends leadership development programs, or seeks feedback from peers is constantly evolving and refining their approach. This growth makes them more adaptable and resilient, qualities that are essential in the fast-paced world of leadership.

Equally important is fostering the growth of others. A leader who actively supports the development of their team members helps to build a more capable, motivated, and engaged workforce. Leaders who invest in their team's growth—whether through training, mentoring, or giving them opportunities to take on new challenges—empower their employees to develop new skills and achieve personal and professional milestones. For example, a leader who encourages a team member to take on a leadership role in a project or enroll in a specialized training program is contributing to their growth. As employees develop, they contribute more effectively to the team's objectives, enhancing overall organizational performance. Moreover, when team members feel that their growth is supported, they are more likely to stay with the organization and contribute to its success over the long term.

The *give–get–grow* cycle in leadership fosters a culture of collaboration, trust, and continuous improvement. Leaders who give by supporting and empowering others, get by being open to feedback, ideas, and support, and grow by investing in their own and others' development create an environment where growth is a collective effort. This cycle promotes mutual benefit, as each person within the organization contributes to and benefits from the growth of others. The more leaders give, the more they foster an environment where others feel inspired to contribute. The more leaders get, the more they learn and adapt, strengthening their leadership abilities. The more leaders and teams grow together, the more they enhance the organization's resilience, innovation, and overall success.

A practical example of this cycle at work can be seen in a leadership team within a nonprofit organization. A leader may give by offering their time and resources to mentor junior staff, sharing their expertise, and providing emotional support. In turn, they receive feedback from staff members on how to improve organizational processes, or support from board members on strategic decisions. The leader's commitment to growing personally through continuous learning enables them to better serve their team. Simultaneously, the leader fosters a culture of growth by providing staff with opportunities to grow in their roles, whether through training programs, increased responsibility, or opportunities for advancement. As a result, the entire organization benefits from a culture of giving, receiving, and growing, leading to enhanced collaboration, innovation, and impact.

In conclusion, leadership through the *give–get–grow* cycle emphasizes the interdependent nature of leadership, where leaders not only give to their teams but are also open to receiving support and feedback, and prioritize growth—both for themselves and for others. This holistic approach to leadership creates an environment of trust, continuous improvement, and mutual benefit, allowing organizations to thrive in an ever-evolving world. Effective leadership is not a solitary pursuit but a dynamic process in which giving, receiving, and growing work together to drive collective success.

Leadership as a Continuous Cycle of Growth

Leadership as a continuous cycle of growth emphasizes that effective leadership is not a fixed destination but an ongoing journey. Successful leaders recognize that their development is never complete, and that their ability to inspire, guide, and support others is continuously evolving. This perspective highlights the importance of self-awareness, adaptability, and the willingness to learn and grow both personally and professionally. Leadership, in this sense, becomes a dynamic process that involves a constant feedback loop of self-improvement, reflection, and innovation. By embracing this mindset, leaders can not only enhance their own abilities but also foster a culture of growth and development within their teams and organizations.

One of the key elements of leadership as a continuous cycle of growth is the ability to reflect and learn from experience. Leaders who prioritize self-reflection are more likely to identify their strengths and weaknesses, which allows them to adjust their approach accordingly. For example, after leading a project that didn't achieve the desired results, a reflective leader would take the time to analyze what went wrong and why. They may recognize that they could have communicated more effectively with their team or that they didn't manage expectations well with stakeholders. By understanding the areas where they could improve, the leader can adjust their strategy for future projects, becoming better equipped to handle similar challenges. This continuous learning process is vital for leadership growth because it turns failures and setbacks into opportunities for improvement.

Leadership growth is also driven by a commitment to learning from others. Effective leaders actively seek out feedback, mentorship, and diverse perspectives to expand their knowledge and skills. For example, a leader in a fast-paced tech company may regularly attend industry conferences, listen to podcasts, or participate in peer networks to stay informed about emerging trends and best practices. They might also engage with other leaders in different fields to gain fresh insights on leadership approaches. By exposing themselves to a variety of ideas and perspectives, these leaders can adapt and innovate their leadership style to meet the evolving needs of their teams and organizations. This openness to learning from others ensures that leadership practices remain relevant and effective, especially in industries that are undergoing rapid change.

Another vital aspect of leadership as a continuous cycle of growth is the ability to cultivate growth in others. Great leaders understand that their success is inherently linked to the development of their team members. As such, they prioritize the personal and professional growth of those they lead, creating opportunities for learning, skill-building, and advancement. For example, a leader may offer a promising team member the opportunity to lead a small project or take on additional responsibilities that align with their career aspirations. By encouraging team members to stretch their abilities, the leader helps them grow, which in turn strengthens the overall team and organization. Furthermore, leaders who foster growth in others are often rewarded with higher levels of engagement, job satisfaction, and loyalty from their team.

This growth mindset also involves adapting leadership styles to fit the needs of the individuals and the situation at hand. For instance, a leader might take a more hands-on, directive approach when leading a new team or working on a project with tight deadlines. However, as the team becomes more experienced or the project enters a more stable phase, the leader might shift to a more collaborative, empowering approach. Leaders who can recognize when to adjust their style based on circumstances and individual team members' needs demonstrate flexibility, which is crucial for ongoing growth. This adaptability is an essential part of leadership development, as it helps leaders respond to changing environments and new challenges without losing effectiveness.

The continuous cycle of growth also encompasses the development of emotional intelligence, which is essential for effective leadership. Leaders who grow in their emotional intelligence are able to manage their emotions, build stronger relationships, and navigate conflicts in a more constructive manner. For instance, a leader who remains calm and empathetic during a team crisis can inspire confidence and reassure their team members. They might also take the time to understand the emotions and motivations of others, which allows them to respond with greater sensitivity and insight. As emotional intelligence grows, leaders become better equipped to create a supportive work environment that fosters collaboration, innovation, and trust. This emotional growth not only benefits the leader but also enhances the overall team dynamic and productivity.

The importance of continuous growth in leadership is also reflected in the ability to foster innovation and inspire others to think creatively. Leaders who grow by encouraging creativity, exploring new ideas, and being open to experimentation help create a culture of innovation. For example, a leader who regularly challenges their team to think outside the box, try new approaches, or collaborate with others across departments will inspire greater creativity and problem-solving. This kind of leadership drives innovation and ensures that the organization is adaptable and competitive in a constantly changing marketplace. By fostering a growth environment that values experimentation and learning from mistakes, leaders encourage their teams to take calculated risks and find innovative solutions to challenges.

Moreover, a leader's commitment to growth can be seen in their efforts to build a resilient team that can weather setbacks and remain focused on long-term goals. Resilience is a key trait that can be developed through consistent leadership growth. For example, during a period of economic downturn or organizational challenges, a leader who demonstrates resilience by maintaining a positive outlook and encouraging their team to stay focused on the mission can help the organization remain motivated and productive. By growing in their own resilience, leaders set an example for their teams and help them develop the perseverance needed to overcome obstacles.

In conclusion, leadership as a continuous cycle of growth is about maintaining a mindset of constant improvement, learning from both successes and failures, and fostering an environment where growth is a collective endeavor. Leaders who prioritize their own growth, seek out feedback, adapt their leadership style, and encourage the development of others create a culture of continuous learning and innovation. This cycle of growth enhances both the individual leader's capabilities and the overall success of the organization. Leadership, when viewed as a continuous cycle, is not a destination but an evolving journey that requires commitment, adaptability, and a dedication to both personal and collective growth.

CHAPTER 12

The Power of Community in the *Give–Get–Grow* Cycle

The power of community in the *give–get–grow* cycle lies in the collective energy, support, and shared growth that emerge when individuals come together with a common purpose. In this cycle, community members engage in a dynamic process of giving, receiving, and growing, each step reinforcing the others to create a strong, thriving group. Communities, whether within a family, a workplace, or a broader social network, are essential for fostering personal and collective development. When individuals within a community give their time, resources, and expertise, they contribute to the overall well-being and success of others. In turn, as they receive support and knowledge, they continue to grow, which not only benefits them but also contributes to the growth of the community itself. This mutual exchange creates an ecosystem of trust, collaboration, and empowerment, where everyone plays a vital role in nurturing each other's development.

For example, in a professional setting, a community of colleagues might share resources, insights, and mentorship with one another. A senior employee may give guidance to a junior colleague, offering advice and sharing experiences to help them navigate challenges and progress in their career. In exchange, the junior employee might offer fresh ideas, new perspectives, or technical skills that can help the senior colleague with ongoing projects. As both individuals give and get from each other, they experience personal growth, gaining confidence, knowledge, and skills that benefit their individual development and, by extension, the success of the organization.

In a community-oriented educational setting, the *give–get–grow* cycle also thrives. For instance, in a study group, participants may give their time to help others understand difficult concepts, provide encouragement during stressful periods, and share their learning materials. In turn, they receive new insights and a sense of accomplishment when their peers benefit from their contributions. Over time, this exchange creates an environment where all members grow—both intellectually and socially—strengthening the group as a whole. This collaborative learning not only enhances the academic success of the individuals involved but also cultivates a deeper sense of connection and belonging within the community.

Another powerful example of community in the *give–get–grow* cycle can be found in volunteer or service-based communities. Individuals who give their time and efforts to causes they care about not only support those in need but also experience personal growth. They might develop new skills, broaden their perspectives, and gain a sense of fulfillment from making a positive impact. As these volunteers work alongside others, they engage in reciprocal relationships where giving and receiving support foster growth. For example, a community organizer might give their time to coordinate efforts for a local environmental cause, but in doing so, they receive valuable lessons about leadership, problem-solving, and the power of collaboration. This experience grows their sense of purpose and increases their ability to influence change in their community.

In the broader societal context, community-based movements or grassroots organizations demonstrate the transformative potential of the *give–get–grow* cycle. When individuals come together around a shared vision for change, each person brings something unique to the table—skills, ideas, resources, or networks. As they give to the cause, they also receive support from one another, forming connections that drive personal growth and strengthen the movement. For example, in a community advocating for environmental sustainability, people might share their knowledge of green technologies, offer their time to clean up local areas, or provide funding to support eco-friendly projects. In return, they gain a sense of purpose, new skills, and a deeper understanding of how to create lasting change. As the community grows stronger, so does the movement, resulting in both individual and collective progress.

Overall, the *give–get–grow* cycle within a community creates a self-sustaining loop where giving leads to receiving, and receiving leads to growth, which in turn strengthens the community as a whole. This dynamic fosters mutual respect, trust, and collaboration, enabling individuals to thrive in an environment that values their contributions and encourages ongoing development. Whether in professional, educational, volunteer, or social settings, the power of community in this cycle is undeniable—it creates a foundation for personal growth, fosters collective progress, and builds stronger, more resilient groups. The more individuals give to and receive from their community, the more they grow, contributing to a vibrant ecosystem where everyone has the opportunity to succeed.

The Foundation of a Thriving Community

The foundation of a thriving community is built on core values such as trust, communication, mutual respect, and shared purpose. These elements create an environment where individuals feel supported, valued, and motivated to contribute to the collective well-being of the group. When these foundational principles are established, they not only foster individual growth but also strengthen the community as a whole, allowing it to flourish and adapt to challenges over time. A thriving community is one where people come together not only for their own benefit but to improve the lives of others, creating a positive feedback loop of support, growth, and shared success.

Trust is one of the most fundamental elements of a thriving community. When people trust each other, they are more likely to engage in open and honest communication, collaborate effectively, and share resources without fear of exploitation. For example, in a workplace, if employees trust their leadership and one another, they are more likely to share innovative ideas, take risks, and work together toward common goals. This trust fosters a culture of transparency where individuals feel safe to express their opinions and take ownership of their work, knowing they have the support of their colleagues. Likewise, in a neighborhood setting, trust between residents can lead to cooperative efforts in community improvement, such as organizing local events, supporting one another during difficult times, and collectively addressing issues such as crime or lack of resources.

Communication is another cornerstone of a thriving community. Effective communication ensures that everyone is aligned with the group's values, goals, and needs. In a community where communication is open, clear, and consistent, misunderstandings are minimized, and people are more likely to feel heard and understood. For instance, in an educational setting, teachers who maintain transparent communication with both students and parents help foster an environment of trust and cooperation. Students feel more confident in their learning when they understand expectations, receive constructive feedback, and know that their concerns will be addressed. Similarly, in volunteer-based organizations, clear communication about roles, expectations, and goals helps individuals feel confident in their contributions and fosters a sense of purpose within the group.

Mutual respect plays a crucial role in maintaining harmony and unity within a thriving community. When individuals respect one another's differences—whether they be cultural, ideological, or experiential—they create an inclusive environment where all voices are valued. This respect fosters a sense of belonging, which is essential for community engagement and participation. In a multicultural community, for example, respect for diverse backgrounds can lead to shared celebrations of different cultural traditions, mutual learning, and greater empathy. As members of the community respect each other's experiences and perspectives, they create opportunities for richer collaboration, leading to more creative solutions and stronger bonds between individuals.

A shared sense of purpose or common goals is vital for a community to thrive. When individuals understand and are aligned with the vision of the community, they are more likely to invest their time, energy, and resources into achieving that vision. For instance, in a business or organizational community, a shared sense of purpose can be seen in employees working together to achieve a common goal, such as improving customer satisfaction or innovating new products. When everyone is on the same page and understands the larger mission, they work more efficiently and with greater enthusiasm. Similarly, in a neighborhood association, when residents are united by a shared goal—such as creating a safer environment or improving public amenities—they are more likely to work together, pool their resources, and actively participate in the planning and execution of community projects.

Shared responsibility is also an important factor in creating a thriving community. When members of a community feel responsible for the well-being of the group as a whole, they are more likely to take ownership of the collective success and contribute meaningfully. In a cooperative business, for example, employees may share responsibility for decision making and the overall success of the company, resulting in greater investment in the organization's success. In a residential community, shared responsibility could mean working together to maintain public spaces, promote environmental sustainability, or assist those in need. When individuals recognize that their actions impact the whole group, they are more likely to be proactive in contributing to the community's needs.

Finally, resilience is a foundational quality that enables communities to endure and thrive in the face of challenges. Resilient communities are able to adapt to changes, bounce back from adversity, and continue progressing even during tough times. For example, in times of natural disasters or economic downturns, a resilient community can pull together to provide support for those affected, rebuild, and find innovative solutions to problems. Resilience in a community is often built through strong social networks, effective communication, and shared problem-solving. When individuals feel supported and connected, they are more likely to persevere through hardship and emerge stronger as a community.

In conclusion, the foundation of a thriving community is built on trust, communication, mutual respect, shared purpose, inclusion, shared responsibility, and resilience. These elements create an environment where individuals are motivated to contribute, grow, and support one another. By fostering a culture that emphasizes these principles, communities can not only enhance the individual well-being of their members but also achieve collective success. Whether in a workplace, a neighborhood, or a broader social network, the strength of a community lies in its ability to bring people together, support one another, and work toward common goals, ensuring that all members can thrive and grow.

The Role of Giving in Community Development

The role of giving in community development is crucial as it fosters a sense of solidarity, mutual support, and shared responsibility. Giving in a community can take many forms, including offering time, resources, knowledge, or skills. When individuals and organizations give to their communities, they contribute to the social fabric that holds the community together, helping to address local challenges, strengthen relationships, and create lasting, positive change. Giving not only benefits those who receive but also enhances the giver's sense of purpose and connection to the broader community, thereby reinforcing the collective well-being and resilience.

For instance, when community members volunteer their time to help with local initiatives—such as organizing a neighborhood cleanup, running youth mentorship programs, or supporting food banks—they directly contribute to improving the environment and the lives of others. Volunteers who give their time and efforts help create a more vibrant, connected, and well-maintained community, which can, in turn, encourage others to give back as well. For example, a neighborhood cleanup initiative can make public spaces safer and more enjoyable, fostering a sense of pride among residents and encouraging them to take better care of their shared environment. Over time, these acts of giving create a cycle of positive change, where individuals feel a deeper connection to the community and are more likely to contribute again.

Giving resources is another powerful aspect of community development. This can include donating money, food, clothes, or other necessities to those in need. Local businesses, charitable organizations, and individuals can come together to provide tangible support to vulnerable community members, such as low-income families, homeless individuals, or those affected by disasters. For example, a local business may donate a portion of its profits to a community development project, such as building affordable housing or funding educational programs for underprivileged children. These contributions can significantly improve the quality of life for community members and provide them with the resources they need to thrive. Moreover, when resources are shared among community members, it creates a sense of interdependence, where everyone plays a role in the overall well-being of the group.

Additionally, the giving of knowledge and skills can be transformative in community development. Many communities face challenges not just due to a lack of resources, but because of limited access to education, expertise, or opportunities for personal growth. When skilled individuals—such as teachers, professionals, or experts in a particular field—give their knowledge and time to others, they help elevate the entire community.

For example, a retired professional may volunteer to offer financial literacy workshops to help community members better manage their finances, or a local artist may provide free art classes to children in underserved neighborhoods. By sharing their expertise, these individuals empower others, giving them the tools and skills they need to improve their lives and contribute more effectively to their community. This exchange of knowledge also strengthens relationships within the community, as it encourages collaboration and learning among diverse groups.

The role of giving in community development also extends to the emotional and social aspects of growth. By showing kindness, empathy, and support, individuals help foster a sense of belonging and security within the community. This emotional support can be seen in neighbors helping each other with childcare, offering a listening ear during difficult times, or providing a safe space for people to express their feelings. For example, a community member who notices a family struggling with illness might offer to help with household chores or bring over a meal, thereby easing the burden and showing care. Such acts of emotional giving contribute to building stronger, more resilient communities where individuals feel valued and connected. Emotional support, though less tangible than financial or physical contributions, is vital for creating a culture of trust and care, where people are motivated to give and help one another.

In larger scale community development projects, such as urban renewal or disaster recovery efforts, collective giving becomes an essential tool for long-term success. For example, after a natural disaster, communities often see an outpouring of support from both local and external sources. Donations in the form of supplies, financial aid, and volunteer labor help rebuild homes, restore public infrastructure, and provide immediate relief to affected residents. However, the ongoing success of recovery efforts requires more than just short-term giving. It requires the sustained investment of time, effort, and resources to rebuild and strengthen the community over time. For example, after the initial disaster recovery, members of the community may give their time to help others rebuild homes, assist in finding employment for those displaced, or organize long-term initiatives that promote economic growth and stability.

Giving also plays an essential role in empowering community members to take ownership of their own development. By providing the tools, support, and resources needed for individuals to succeed, communities can create a sense of agency and self-determination. For example, community-driven development projects often rely on individuals giving their time and knowledge to identify local needs and implement solutions. When people are involved in the decision-making process and feel that their contributions matter, they become more invested in the success of the community and its development. Whether it's a neighborhood association working together to improve public spaces or a group of volunteers coming together to create a local after-school program, the act of giving not only supports immediate needs but also empowers individuals to contribute to the broader vision of community growth.

In conclusion, giving plays an indispensable role in community development by fostering connection, support, and shared responsibility. Whether through offering time, resources, knowledge, or emotional support, giving strengthens the social bonds within a community and creates a cycle of positive change. By encouraging acts of generosity and service, communities become more resilient, self-sustaining, and capable of addressing both immediate and long-term challenges. As individuals give to one another, they not only contribute to the well-being of others but also experience personal growth, creating a thriving community where everyone's needs are met, and collective success is achieved.

The Role of Getting in Community Development

The role of getting in community development is equally important as giving, as it fosters mutual growth, collaboration, and the exchange of resources and ideas. Getting, in the context of community development, refers to receiving support, knowledge, resources, and opportunities that allow individuals and groups to improve themselves, their circumstances, and the community as a whole. When individuals are open to receiving, they not only enhance their own development but also contribute to the overall health and sustainability of the community by ensuring that the cycle of give-and-take continues. This exchange is essential in creating a dynamic, responsive community where needs are met, potential is maximized, and progress is made.

One way that getting plays a significant role in community development is through the access to resources that individuals or groups may lack. For example, a family struggling with financial hardship may rely on local charities or government assistance programs for food, shelter, or health care. Through these programs, individuals "get" the resources they need to improve their circumstances, allowing them to regain their footing and eventually give back to the community once they are more stable. This cycle of receiving and then contributing back is essential for creating a resilient community where no one is left behind. When people receive support, whether financial, emotional, or practical, it enables them to move toward self-sufficiency, and in turn, they may offer their help to others when they are in a better position to do so.

Another example of the role of getting in community development is the importance of receiving knowledge and training to empower individuals. In many communities, particularly those facing economic or educational challenges, access to education and skill-building programs is key to personal and community growth. By receiving education or professional development training, individuals can acquire skills that not only improve their own prospects but also enhance the community's ability to thrive. For example, individuals who participate in vocational training programs to learn new trades can gain employment, thus improving their own quality of life and contributing to the local economy. Over time, they may return to the community as mentors or trainers, sharing the skills they've acquired with others, thus perpetuating the cycle of giving and receiving.

In addition, getting in community development often involves receiving emotional and social support. A key aspect of any thriving community is the ability to lean on others during times of personal or collective hardship. Whether through formal counseling programs, peer support groups, or informal networks of friends and neighbors, receiving emotional support strengthens individuals' resilience and helps them overcome challenges. For example, a person who has experienced loss may find comfort and healing by receiving emotional support from friends or a support group. This, in turn, can enable them to contribute to the community's well-being in the future by offering support to others in similar situations. The sharing of emotional and psychological support within a community helps build trust, empathy, and a deeper sense of belonging.

Moreover, getting can be a critical part of creating opportunities for leadership and participation. When individuals within a community receive opportunities to participate in decision-making processes or leadership roles, they can help shape the direction of the community's development. For instance, a community group working on a neighborhood beautification project might invite members to participate in planning meetings, share their ideas, and take on leadership roles in organizing events. By receiving the opportunity to contribute in meaningful ways, individuals not only enhance their personal growth and leadership skills but also ensure that the community's development is informed by the diverse needs and perspectives of its members. This sense of ownership and involvement encourages greater investment in the success of the community as a whole.

Additionally, the role of getting in community development extends to the access individuals have to networks and connections. A person who gets connected to a network of professionals, mentors, or like-minded community members may find new career opportunities, gain access to new markets for their business, or receive advice and guidance that helps them make better decisions. For example, a small business owner in a community may join a local business association, where they receive mentoring from more experienced entrepreneurs. These new connections can help them expand their business, create jobs, and contribute to the local economy. As the individual's success grows, they may, in turn, help other small business owners or aspiring entrepreneurs, continuing the cycle of support and growth.

The reciprocal nature of giving and getting also plays a vital role in fostering inclusivity and unity within communities. When people are open to receiving assistance or opportunities, it promotes a culture of reciprocity, where individuals understand that their success is intertwined with the success of others. For instance, in a diverse community, newcomers may receive help adjusting to the local culture, navigating the language, or finding employment. As they get settled and integrate, they may then give back by sharing their own knowledge and experiences, enriching the community with new perspectives, traditions, or talents. This cycle of getting and giving ensures that all members, regardless of their background or circumstances, have the opportunity to contribute to and benefit from the community's collective growth.

In conclusion, the role of getting involved in community development is vital for ensuring that individuals and groups have the necessary resources, knowledge, and support to grow and thrive. By being open to receiving help, individuals not only enhance their own lives but also strengthen the community by contributing to its resilience, diversity, and collective progress. The cycle of give-and-get creates a dynamic and interconnected community where everyone has the opportunity to flourish. Whether through accessing resources, gaining knowledge, receiving emotional support, or participating in leadership, getting plays an essential part in both personal and community development.

The Role of Growing in Community Development

The role of growing in community development is essential as it ensures that individuals and communities continue to evolve, adapt, and thrive in an ever-changing world. Growth in this context refers to the continuous improvement and expansion of skills, knowledge, resources, and social connections that benefit both individuals and the community at large. Growing within a community involves both personal development and collective progress, where everyone's efforts contribute to the overall success of the group. The process of growing not only enhances the capabilities of individuals but also strengthens the community by fostering innovation, resilience, and long-term sustainability.

One of the most direct ways that growth contributes to community development is through the improvement of skills and capabilities among its members. When individuals grow personally—whether by acquiring new job skills, pursuing education, or developing leadership abilities—they are better equipped to contribute to the community's needs. For example, a local resident who participates in a job training program or earns a degree in a high-demand field may gain access to higher-paying jobs and improve their standard of living. As they progress in their careers, they may also help others by offering mentorship, contributing to the local economy, or advocating for improvements in community services. This cycle of personal growth leading to community growth helps elevate the overall well-being of the entire group, creating a more prosperous and connected environment.

Similarly, growing in the context of community development also involves the sharing and exchange of knowledge. A community that values learning and growth encourages its members to constantly seek opportunities to expand their understanding of issues, resources, and best practices. For example, a community that prioritizes educational development might establish local schools, after-school programs, or adult education initiatives to help people of all ages acquire new knowledge. In turn, the individuals who gain this knowledge can share it with others, whether through teaching, training, or community workshops. For instance, a local farmer who learns new sustainable agricultural practices might pass this knowledge along to others in the community, improving farming techniques and environmental stewardship for everyone. The collective growth of knowledge within a community creates a culture of continuous learning and improvement, ensuring that members are always equipped to face future challenges and opportunities.

The process of growing also encourages innovation within a community. Communities that foster an environment of creativity and experimentation tend to be more adaptable and capable of solving complex problems. For example, a neighborhood that promotes innovation may see its residents come together to develop solutions for local challenges, such as waste management, public transportation, or public safety. Community-driven initiatives, such as establishing urban gardens, implementing green energy projects, or creating coworking spaces, are examples of growth that stem from the collective creativity and resourcefulness of community members. As people grow in their ability to think critically and creatively, they contribute to solutions that benefit the community as a whole, addressing issues in novel and sustainable ways.

Community growth also involves the development of social networks and relationships that support personal and collective well-being. Social capital—referring to the networks of relationships and trust between individuals—plays a crucial role in how well a community can grow and adapt. For example, a community that has strong social ties is better able to respond to crises, whether they are natural disasters, economic recessions, or public health emergencies. When individuals and families know they can rely on their neighbors for support, they are more likely to engage in community-building activities that promote collective well-being.

Community events, social gatherings, or volunteer projects can all foster relationships and create a supportive environment where people feel connected to one another. These connections help individuals grow emotionally and socially, as they know that they are part of a larger group working toward common goals. Moreover, as relationships deepen, the sense of belonging within the community strengthens, making people more invested in its growth and success.

The role of growing in community development also extends to the evolution of community infrastructure and public services. As communities grow and change, there is a need for improved infrastructure to meet the evolving demands of residents. For example, as a city's population increases, there may be a growing demand for more schools, hospitals, transportation systems, and recreational spaces. Community members and local governments must work together to ensure that growth is sustainable and that infrastructure can accommodate the changing needs of the population. When people grow in their understanding of community planning and development, they can contribute ideas and solutions to create a more livable and efficient environment. In some cases, the community might even engage in participatory planning, where residents take an active role in designing the future of their neighborhoods or cities. Through this collaborative process, the community can grow in a way that ensures long-term success and addresses both current and future needs.

Finally, the role of growing in community development is intertwined with sustainability. As communities grow, it is important to ensure that growth is environmentally and economically sustainable, so that future generations can continue to thrive. For example, a community that invests in renewable energy, eco-friendly transportation, and sustainable agriculture is growing in a way that considers the long-term health of the environment. Additionally, communities that focus on economic sustainability—by supporting local businesses, creating job opportunities, and fostering entrepreneurial spirit—ensure that their growth benefits everyone in the community and does not come at the expense of future generations. By growing in ways that are sustainable, communities can create a lasting legacy of success and resilience.

In conclusion, growing is an essential aspect of community development, as it enables individuals and groups to continuously improve, adapt, and innovate in response to changing circumstances. Whether it involves acquiring new skills, sharing knowledge, fostering social connections, building infrastructure, or pursuing sustainability, growth ensures that communities are better equipped to face challenges and seize opportunities. The process of growing within a community creates a cycle of improvement that benefits everyone, leading to stronger, more resilient, and more prosperous communities.

The Infinite Potential of a Thriving Community

In conclusion, the infinite potential of a thriving community lies in the powerful, ongoing cycle of *give–get–grow*. This principle, when embraced by every individual and collective effort, creates a dynamic force of growth, resilience, and transformation. At its core, the *give–get–grow* cycle is about reciprocal relationships that uplift individuals and empower the collective to reach new heights. It is a continuous loop where each act of giving leads to receiving, and each opportunity for growth fosters further contribution. It is in this endless cycle that communities find their true potential—ever evolving, always expanding, and forever united by a shared purpose.

Consider a community that, despite initial challenges, begins to invest in its people—encouraging them to give their time, resources, and expertise to one another. From local mentorship programs to community gardens that provide food for all, these acts of giving create ripple effects that strengthen the bonds within the group. But the magic happens when people open themselves up to receive: receiving support, knowledge, and opportunities that help them thrive. Imagine a young person from a low-income neighborhood receiving a scholarship from a local business or a small entrepreneur gaining the mentorship they need to scale their venture. By receiving, they not only elevate their own lives but also enrich the community with new ideas, energy, and commitment.

As these individuals grow in their abilities, confidence, and aspirations, the community grows too—becoming a stronger, more innovative, and inclusive place. People who were once recipients of help become the givers, passing on their knowledge, resources, and support to others. This cycle repeats itself, deepening the community's roots and expanding its horizons. A small group of volunteers may start by cleaning a local park, but over time, their collective efforts may lead to the development of a community center, new local businesses, or even policy changes that benefit everyone. In this way, growth becomes not just an individual achievement but a shared victory, where everyone's contributions make a tangible difference.

Take, for example, a city that faced significant economic decline but, through a commitment to giving, receiving, and growing, transformed itself into a hub of innovation and collaboration. Local residents gave their time to support job training programs, small businesses helped each other thrive, and nonprofits worked tirelessly to empower individuals with education and resources. As people received the tools they needed to succeed, they grew—personally, professionally, and as members of a greater community. Over time, that city became a symbol of how communities can rise from hardship through collective action. The businesses, residents, and organizations, once struggling, now shared in the prosperity they had created together.

The true beauty of the *give–get–grow* principle lies in its adaptability and scalability. Whether in a small rural town or a sprawling metropolis, this cycle can create lasting change when individuals and groups are committed to contributing, receiving, and evolving. It teaches us that no contribution is too small and that everyone's growth has a direct impact on the growth of others. In a thriving community, the success of one is celebrated by all, and the struggles of one are shouldered by all. This is the spirit of true community—the idea that we are all connected, and that by uplifting each other, we build something greater than ourselves.

As we look to the future, we must hold onto the vision of a community where every individual can flourish, and in doing so, help others do the same. The infinite potential of a thriving community is not a distant dream—it is within our grasp, fueled by the simple yet profound principle of *give–get–grow*. When we give of ourselves, when we open ourselves to receive, and when we commit to growing together, we unlock the boundless possibilities for collective success. It's a cycle that can transform lives, heal divides, and build a world where every community is not only surviving but thriving—together. The power is within us all, and the journey begins now.

A Note of Thanks

As I reach the conclusion of this book, I want to take a moment to express my deepest gratitude to those who have helped make *The Power of Community: Give, Get, and Grow* a reality.

First and foremost, my heartfelt thanks go to my parents, whose love, wisdom, and selflessness have shaped not only my life but the essence of this book. Their actions have been a constant source of inspiration, and it is through their example that I have learned the true power of community—one that thrives on giving, receiving, and growing together. I can only hope to pass on even a fraction of their generosity and kindness through the pages of this work.

A heartfelt thanks to my son, Aayush Kumar for being my inspiration to fulfill my dreams. For always being there and offering support every time I need it. For being the biggest critic and encouraging to think from all perspectives to most of my out-of-the-box thoughts.

A special thanks to Jim Spohrer as my mentor and the ISSIP (International Society of Service Innovation Professionals) Community Leader for the constant encouragement to push me in making this book a reality. To my friends, other mentors and community members who have supported me along this journey: Your encouragement and belief in me have been invaluable. Each conversation, each shared experience, has enriched this book and deepened my understanding of what it means to give and grow within a community.

A special thank-you to my readers. It is your engagement and your willingness to explore the power of community that drives me forward. May this book inspire you to find your own unique ways of giving, receiving, and growing with others. Together, we can create a world where the spirit of kindness, support, and connection flourishes.

Lastly, I would like to express my gratitude to the unsung heroes—those who work quietly, without seeking recognition, to make the world a better place. Your impact is immeasurable, and it is my hope that through this book, we can all be reminded of the power we each have to make a difference in the lives of those around us.

Thank you for being part of this journey, and may the lessons of giving, getting, and growing continue to guide us all.

With gratitude and appreciation,
Vaishali Mane

Bibliography

1. Putnam, Robert D. *Bowling Alone: The Collapse and Revival of American Community.* Simon & Schuster, 2000.
    - A seminal work that explores the decline of social capital in America and the impact of community involvement on societal well-being.
2. Wenger, Etienne, Richard McDermott, and William Snyder. *Cultivating Communities of Practice: A Guide to Managing Knowledge.* Harvard Business Press, 2002.
    - A comprehensive guide on creating and sustaining communities of practice to enhance collective knowledge and growth.
3. Seligman, Martin E. P. *Flourish: A Visionary New Understanding of Happiness and Well-Being.* Free Press, 2011.
    - Explores the link between individual and collective well-being and how thriving communities contribute to happiness.
4. Brown, Brené. *Braving the Wilderness: The Quest for True Belonging and the Courage to Stand Alone.* Random House, 2017.
    - Discusses the importance of belonging, vulnerability, and creating strong communities, while navigating the tension between individuality and connection.
5. Hawkins, David A. *The Power of Giving: How Giving Back Creates a Better World.* Hay House, 2006.
    - Explores how acts of giving within communities have the potential to improve lives and create lasting, positive change.
6. Klein, Naomi. *The Shock Doctrine: The Rise of Disaster Capitalism.* Metropolitan Books, 2007.
    - Although primarily a critique of global capitalism, it includes insights on how communities are affected by external forces and the importance of collective resilience.
7. Cohen, Jean L., and Andrew Arato. *Civil Society and Political Theory.* MIT Press, 1992.
    - A philosophical exploration of how communities form and the role of civil society in political life.
8. McMillan, David W., and David M. Chavis. "Sense of Community: A Definition and Theory." *Journal of Community Psychology* 14, no. 1 (1986): 6–23.
    - A foundational academic article that presents a model of what constitutes a "sense of community" and its role in social relationships.

9. Tönnies, Ferdinand. *Community and Society (Gemeinschaft und Gesellschaft)*. Dover Publications, 2001 (Original work published in 1887).
   - A classic sociological work that distinguishes between two types of social groups: "Gemeinschaft" (community) and "Gesellschaft" (society).
10. McKnight, John, and Peter Block. *The Abundant Community: Awakening the Power of Families and Neighborhoods*. Berrett-Koehler Publishers, 2010.
   - This book emphasizes the importance of local communities and how they can transform the lives of their members through cooperation and shared purpose.
11. Berkes, Fikret, and Carl Folke, eds. *Sacrificing the Commons: Sustainability and Community-Based Resource Management*. Cambridge University Press, 1998.
   - Examines the role of community-based resource management in achieving sustainability, with a focus on collective action and cooperation.
12. Chavis, David M., and Kien Lee. *Creating Community: An Action-Oriented Approach to Community Building*. New Community Press, 2015.
   - A practical guide to the steps involved in building and maintaining strong, effective communities.
13. Gergen, Kenneth J. *Relational Being: Beyond Self and Community*. Oxford University Press, 2009.
   - A philosophical exploration of the concept of community from the perspective of relational psychology.
14. Hochschild, Arlie Russell. *The Managed Heart: Commercialization of Human Feeling*. University of California Press, 1983.
   - Discusses how emotional labor and the commercialization of relationships impact community building, particularly in the workplace.
15. Tanner, Laura. *Radical Care: Surviving the Plague of Individualism*. University of California Press, 2022.
   - Explores how care practices, particularly in the context of community and collective survival, can radically reshape social interactions.
16. Sanders, Mark. *The Giving Tree: A Story About Love and Generosity*. HarperCollins, 1964.
   - A beloved children's book that reflects the theme of selfless giving and the power of generosity in relationships.
17. The Center for Nonprofit Excellence. *Building Community Capacity: Effective Strategies for Organizing Groups for Action*. Wiley, 2003.
   - Provides insight into organizing community groups to effectively address local needs and create positive change.

18. Wheatley, Margaret J. *Leadership and the New Science: Discovering Order in a Chaotic World.* Berrett-Koehler Publishers, 2006.
    ○ Explores how concepts from new science can inform the way communities grow, evolve, and interact, especially under challenging circumstances.

About the Author

Vaishali Mane holds a master's degree from the prestigious Indian Institute of Technology, Madras, with extensive experience in product management, program management, and Agile methodologies. Throughout her career, she has worked with organizations such as Google, F5, Akamai Technologies, Wells Fargo, Charles Schwab, IBM, and IIT Madras. She is known for driving collaboration and fostering innovation.

Beyond her professional accomplishments, Vaishali comes from a deeply rooted, humble, and highly educated family background. Her parents have been her unwavering source of inspiration, instilling in her strong moral values and a commitment to community service. These principles shape her work, contributions, and passion for writing, as well as her unique creative talent. In addition to her professional and creative pursuits, Vaishali cherishes quality time with her loved ones, with family always at the center of her life.

Index

Synergy between personal development and community growth, 151–154

Thriving community, 153
- communication and, 177
- foundation of, 177–179
- mutual respect and, 178
- resilience, 179
- shared responsibility, 178–179
- shared sense of purpose or common goals, 178
- trust and, 177

Trust, 65–66, 159–160
- building, 72–74
- in business relationships, 69, 75
- in community leadership, 81
- cultivating, 74–76
- defined, 66
- in education, 81
- in family dynamics, 82
- in financial transactions, 67
- fragile, 66, 75–76
- mistrust, dangers of, 70–72
- modeling, 80–82
- parent, 70
- in personal relationships, 65–68, 74–75
- and reciprocity, cycle of, 69–70
- in relationship between managers and employees, 80–81
- role of reciprocity in building, 72–74
- social, 67, 75
- in teams, 81
- thriving community and, 177
- and vulnerability, 67–69
- in workplace, 66–67, 70

Urban loneliness, 11

Volunteer, 12, 24, 27–33, 152, 157–158, 176–181, 186–187
- in community projects, 25–26
- contributions, 142
- delivering groceries, 25
- doctor, 19
- efforts, 98
- encouraging, 84, 88
- labor, 181
- to mentor others, 154
- organization, 40, 44, 178
- outreach program, 8
- teaching skill, 142

Vulnerability, 37, 39, 56, 66, 74, 97, 147, 157
- defined, 67–68
- trust and, 67–69

Willingness, 3, 24, 27, 39–41, 67–68, 150–151, 157, 159–160, 162, 165, 170, 191

www.ingramcontent.com/pod-product-compliance
Lightning Source LLC
Chambersburg PA
CBHW061212220326
41599CB00025B/4615